and then there were three...

and then there were three...

a memoir

Supriya Bhatnagar

For: Anjana, with Best wishes, Supriya Oct '10

SERVING HOUSE BOOKS

and then there were three...

ISBN: 978-0-9825462-9-1

Cover photo: N. Satyan

Author photo: AWP

Serving House Books logo by Barry Lereng Wilmont

Published by Serving House Books

www.servinghousebooks.com

First Serving House Books Edition 2010

The unreal has no existence and the real never ceases to be;
The reality of both has thus been perceived by the seers of truth.
—The Bhagvad Gita; 2:16

For my mother
In memory of my father

For Anil, Akshay, Aditya, & Anurag
my knights...

Supriya Bhatnagar is the Director of
Publications for the Association of Writers
& Writing Programs (AWP). Her MFA in
Nonfiction is from George Mason University.
She has published a short story in *Femina*,
a leading English magazine in India, and
"Color," a chapter from her memoir, *And then
there were three...* in *Perigee* and a version of the
chapter "Shattered" in *Artful Dodge*.

Contents

Prologue

Last night I had the same dream again. I dreamt that I smoked a cigarette. I lighted it, brought it to my lips, and inhaled deeply. I felt the smoke going down my throat, that heady smell of tobacco, just before I let the smoke out slowly and deliberately. I saw the rings that came out and the glowing tip of the cigarette that I held delicately between my middle and forefingers.

And then I woke up to hear my husband snoring louder than ever by my side. Anil has never smoked in his life, never had the desire, never tried one either. We tell our three sons now that cigarette smoking is bad. We give them statistics and articles to read. We do it subtly, but we never miss a chance.

Then why do I smoke in my dreams? Why do I do something that in my waking hours I would shun? Friends and family have jokingly quoted Freud, saying that this desire is in my subconscious. I deny this claim vehemently, but it nags me. Why? Do I need Freudian analysis to get to the bottom of this? What am I suppressing?

Daddy was a smoker. Every night after dinner, he would go out on the balcony of our second floor apartment in Bombay, lean on the railing, and enjoy a *Wills*. Mummy would stand next to him, and I could hear them talking leisurely. At that moment they were one, and in my nine-year-old eyes, this picture was the epitome of romance.

My father was not a chain smoker, but he did enjoy a cigarette or two every night. Maybe he smoked in the daytime too. I do not remember. What I remember is his silhouette against the moonlight and the rings of smoke that wafted over his head. What I remember is the way he stuck the cigarette in the corner of his mouth as he inhaled, and his head tilting back as he let the smoke out towards the night sky.

Shattered

O ver the years, I find that I have developed a deep dislike for the month of May. As a child I did not know it, but the feeling was there in my subconscious. As an adult, I can identify this dislike and confront it. I dread its approach, and am relieved when it leaves. Back in 1971, when Shammi was six and I was nine—almost ten, nationalism had not swept through the country yet, and Bombay had not become Mumbai, Calcutta had not become Kolkatta, and Madras had not become Chennai. Bombay was a bustling metropolis, but we lived on the outskirts, in the quiet suburb of Mulund—Mummy, Daddy, Shammi, and I, and as always, the month of May was hot and humid that year. The peace and calm of Mulund matched our family life. We were the comfortable middle class—a nice house, a nice car, a nice husband, a nice wife, and of course, two nice children. In fact, whenever I saw a billboard that advertised family planning showing a nice looking man, a well-dressed woman, and two happy children—a little boy with curly hair and his sister whose pigtails were flying in the air at right angles to her ears—with the caption *Hum Do, Hamaare Do,* which loosely translates as "We are two, we have two," I imagined my family up there. Except that I should have been a boy. Only then would we become perfect.

For my father, it *was* a perfect family. I often found my parents locked in a loving embrace, and much to their delight, I would squeeze in between them, my way of being embarrassed at this intimate scene.

Daddy enjoyed having two girls, though Mummy had wished for at least one boy. "I shall enjoy all the attention from these girls when they grow up," he would tell my mother. When Mummy was expecting me, he was very sure it would be a girl and had even picked out a name, refusing to think of boy names. And when Mummy was expecting my sister, it was the same story all over again.

Mummy often got into trouble because of the intense love that Daddy had for his family. "When you are with your brothers and sisters, you forget to look after my girls," he would complain, annoying her immensely. How can a mother ever forget her children, she would argue. I once walked into their bedroom, and watched with wicked delight as Daddy defended my actions to Mummy after I had supposedly misbehaved in front of my visiting aunt and uncle, saying that, after all, she is only a child. He was on *my* side!

Daddy was particular about keeping himself fit. He would use the *Bullworker*, a long metallic contraption that had flexible bands on either side. You would have to pull at these bands, which was tough, and that would work out the muscles on your arm. After exercising, he would come out of his room in a blue-gray checkered lungi, with a towel draped around his sweating upper body. His stomach was flat, and muscles rippled on his arms. My mother, on the other hand, was comfortably well rounded, and Daddy liked that. He did not like skinny women, he would say, making Mummy very happy. "I would be afraid to hug you so hard," he would joke, giving her a tight squeeze.

Like most Indian marriages, my parents' wedding had been an arranged one. My father's sisters tell me how lovely Mummy looked the day her parents brought her over to meet their family. "We admired her long hair too," they say now, "and then of course found out that it was false," they smile, remembering the occasion. For the meeting, Mummy had bought false hair and weaved it in her own short hair to make a long plait. Daddy was smitten instantly. There was some time between the engagement and the wedding, so they could get to know each other by going out for a movie or for dinner. His reputation as a Casanova had suffered a serious blow when he married my mother—she was smart and very intelligent, but nothing like the ultra-modern girls he met at work and flirted with, and his family was pleasantly surprised and pleased.

All week during that sweltering middle of May, Daddy had been making plans to attend a favorite cousin's wedding out of town. Schools were closed for summer vacation, and Shammi and I had just finished building an elaborate tent made of different colored sheets on our bed, and were busy putting our dolls—our babies—to bed. Daddy had to go into the city for something, and he walked in with Mummy to say goodbye, catching us in the act of nurturing our babies. "Shhhh," I whispered, putting my forefinger on my lips and pointing to my sister. "This is a hospital and she's just had a baby." My parents laughed indulgently. The previous week, we had all gone to the local hospital to see Mrs. Shrivastav's—our neighbor on the floor above ours—new baby, and of course, this was a direct result of that visit.

The next morning, a kind neighbor, who I found out had spent the night in our home, woke us up and asked us to get dressed. "We have to go to the hospital," Suzie Aunty said gently. "Mummy is waiting for you." It was a long and quiet drive to the city, and the hospital was a huge building in the heart of it. I had to look up all the way towards the sky to see the top of the building. We did not use the elevators, but climbed the wide stairwell. Two floors, or three, or four, I lost count. Mummy was waiting for us at the top, her arms outstretched to gather us in her embrace. She cried as we were led into one of the rooms. Big windows let in lots of light, and I saw Mummy's sister sitting on a chair sobbing quietly. Then I saw Daddy lying on the bed. His handsome face was calm, and he was in deep sleep. I knew instinctively that he was dead.

I sat on my aunt's lap, staring at Daddy's face, not yet feeling the impact of his death. I knew something terrible had happened, but then Daddy was still in front of us. Shammi sat on Mummy's lap. A nurse passing by peeped in and wiped tears from her eyes. Was she the one who attended to my father? I looked around the room to see Mrs. Iyer, my father's boss's wife and a good friend of our family, standing in the corner, wiping tears from her eyes. She did not once move from that spot. Just as I had looked up at the hospital from the street, I looked up at the ceiling of the room. It was unusually high, and a white ceiling fan hung from the middle on a long rod. The hospital was a relic of a bygone era, a building built by the British Raj, its distempered walls shining in the sunlight that streamed in. I finally cried, and so did my sister. When it was time to leave, Mummy asked us to kiss Daddy. I leaned over, and when my lips touched his forehead, it was warm.

That was the last time I kissed my father, and as I bent over him, I smelled the familiar scent of his aftershave mingling with the shampoo he had used for his hair.

Once home, friends and family started trickling in. It was strange to see Mummy sitting in the easy chair in her bedroom and crying. Shammi and I sat on her bed not knowing what to say or do, while Thambi, our trusted servant of many years, stood by the door, weeping like a little boy. Everything felt unreal. The living room was cleared of the furniture in preparation for Daddy to come home one last time. Huge slabs of ice were brought in and placed on the floor, and soon his body was carried in and laid on the ice. His head was bandaged, and he was covered up to his neck with a white sheet. Mummy came out of her room then, and sat on a tiny stool by his head.

In India, there is no concept of a funeral parlor. The funeral procession starts from the home, and for Hindus, the body is taken to the cremation *ghat*, a piece of land dedicated for burning funeral pyres. Because of the intense heat, ice is needed to keep the body cold, and this allows time for the relatives to come from out of town. One of my father's older brothers had died when I was a baby, and this was the second tragedy in the family. His mother, my grandmother, was too old to travel to Bombay from Bangalore. Having lost her husband early in life, her youngest son's death was a blow to her fragile body; of her eight children who survived to adulthood, only six were now left.

Daddy's death made me think of another funeral a few months before. It was in the neighboring building, and I had watched with curious eyes. It was a Christian funeral, and I did not know the family well. A white van had backed up to the front steps of the building so the back doors could be opened to let the coffin slide in. The widow followed the coffin, her arms outstretched, weeping inconsolably. A large crowd had gathered to send the dead man off. I had stood on the balcony of our apartment and watched the whole scene as if I were watching a tragedy on the big screen. Now, all of them watched us with curious eyes. I saw faces peering out of every apartment window, pointing and whispering. The apartment was full of people by now, and I spent most of my time on the balcony, as it was distressing to see my mother in this state of despair. Shammi lay on her bed with her face against the wall, refusing to speak to anyone. At six, she seemed to be showing her grief better than I did. As for me, I wandered in once in a while, watching other people's reactions. It was strangely comforting to know that Daddy was still in the house. When one of his older brothers arrived, he bent over Daddy, placing his forehead on that of his lifeless brother for the longest time.

Our apartment in Bombay was on the first floor, which, in India, is one floor above ground level. When it was time for the priest to perform the last rites, Daddy was taken to the ground floor, just outside the building, and I looked down to watch. Mummy stood by me, sobbing uncontrollably. I looked around, and saw everyone watching the rites–sympathetic and grieving faces, and then it was all over. He was gone. One of Daddy's sisters, my Neela

Aunty, arrived soon after the funeral procession left from our home. She had driven from her house a few hours away, and was distraught that she couldn't see her brother one last time. Neela Aunty had always been the bold one. All of us had admired her when she started learning horse riding well into her thirties. And now she showed the same spunk by defying convention and rushing to the *ghat*.

According to Hindu rites, women do not take part in the funeral procession. The oldest son lights the pyre, or in an electric crematorium, as is more often the case these days, he turns the switch on; but in my father's case, in the absence of sons, his older brother lighted the pyre. The third day after the funeral, relatives return to collect the cooled off ashes and the few remaining bones of the body that do not burn, and then immerse them in the waters of some holy river. I do not know what happened to my father's ashes, and am reluctant to ask anyone now. Do I fear stirring up painful memories? Maybe so, or maybe I do not care. His death was a major upheaval in our lives, and while growing up I dealt with it by not questioning anything. It was easy for a nine-year-old to go on with life and lose herself in the daily happenings. I look back now at the logistics of a cremation in a *ghat,* which are mind-boggling. Wood has to be bought for the funeral pyre, along with other items like rice, white cloth, *ghee* (clarified butter), turmeric, *tulsi* (basil leaves), *kumkum* (vermilion powder), milk, incense sticks, etc. But death is also a business like any other, and these days everything can be bought in one consolidated package. It is as easy as that. Or in the case of the middle-class and the wealthy, the flick of a switch at an electric crematorium is all that it takes to send the departed soul to its afterlife.

In his short life, my father had done well for himself. We were comfortable, the ultimate being the ownership of a black Ambassador sedan. What more could we want? My mother loved dressing her girls alike, and our well-dressed selves proved her expert sewing skills. She too looked elegant and beautiful in her lovely saris, and always wore the perfect jewelry for any occasion. My parents had ten years together, and they enjoyed every moment of it. Before my sister was born, my father had gone to Germany for almost a whole year, and I often see the photographs he sent home from there and read his letters addressed to both my mother and me—*my dear girls*, he called us.

In one photograph, he is sitting on his bed, with framed photographs of his "dear girls" on the nightstand. I still cherish the "walkie-talkie" doll he brought me, and I see the photograph in which I carry Lolita—how the doll ended up with this very non-Indian name is a mystery to me, though I suspect now that Daddy must have read Nabokov's *Lolita* in his spare time in Germany—and see that she is half the length of my four-year-old body. She has beautiful transparent blue eyes framed by long curling lashes (her eyelids closed when we made her lie down). She has a full head of the most exotic ivory white hair, and she wears a bright red pinafore with matching red underwear. On her feet are ivory party shoes and socks that have lace on them. I hug the doll close to me, my mouth wide open in a shy smile.

On Lolita's back was a small opening with a ring sticking out. When pulled, something magical happened and Lolita spoke complete sentences in English! I would watch as Mummy made her stand on the ground and then gently pushed down on her left shoulder. Her right leg would move forward and then the right shoulder had to be pushed down for the left leg to move. She could walk! I have not forgotten the particular fragrance of her hard plastic body as I held her close, and often I would peek into her underwear to see how real she actually was. But now however, Lolita is only a link between a dead father and the little girl he doted upon. The passage of time has been kind to Lolita, and she remains in the original red frock she arrived in. Whenever I go home to visit my mother now, I hold her once and smell the quaint fragrance of her hard plastic body, and if no one is watching, I even plant a quick kiss on her chubby cheeks.

After Daddy's death, we had to move out of the apartment. It belonged to Consolidated Pneumatic Tools (CPT) where he worked, and somebody else needed it, upsetting our well-laid out plans. In ten years of married life, Mummy had been busy raising us and looking after the house. Finally, that past year, she had convinced my father that the girls were old enough, and that she would like to work outside the house. So much had happened that summer. My parents had decided that they would transfer us to a new "progressive" school, and by happy coincidence, my mother was offered a teaching position at the very same school. How thrilling to think that all three of us would go to school together each morning! My mother was terribly excited too. She had excelled in her school and college days, and had desperately wanted to be a doctor. My grandfather, however, for reasons unknown, insisted that she should marry soon. Though my father made her very happy, my mother always cherished the dream of a career.

Soon after the funeral, a stranger came and drove our black car away. He was a nice man, and talked very politely. When she saw the car disappearing down the street, Mummy cried. Mummy cried a lot those days, especially when she was packing all our things. Daddy's clothes were going into separate suitcases—his entire cricket stuff too. My father was a wonderful cricket player. He had enjoyed playing the sport in his school and college days, and continued doing so in adulthood. He played for his company's team, and was very popular, more so because he was the only engineer who played. His teammates were blue-collar factory workers whom he treated as his equal. I remember going to the city to watch him play once. He looked so handsome in his white trousers, white shirt, white sneakers, and a sleeveless white woolen vest that had a thin green stripe for a border. My mother, sister, and I sat in the shade of a huge banyan tree, a little away from the pitch. Once, he came home after a game, badly bruised. The cricket ball had hit him hard on his thigh, leaving the area black and blue. My mother rubbed *Iodex* on it for several days after that, and we girls watched the round green spot shrink in size as if by magic.

The mourning period after a Hindu funeral lasts thirteen days. On the thirteenth day, the priest performs special pujas to assist the departed soul's final journey to the afterlife. In those thirteen days, Mummy decided that we were moving to Jaipur where her older sister lived, and Amma, my maternal grandmother, would go with us too. The train ride to Jaipur would be very exciting, I remember thinking. We would be living in a new city, and my sister and I would attend a new school. We would have new uniforms and make new friends, even though I would miss my friends in Bombay. Thambi cried when he heard that we were leaving. He had cooked and cleaned for us for four years now, and Daddy had even seen to it that he had a job in a factory. He didn't want to be left alone in Bombay. Mummy told him that he would have a better life as a factory worker than as a domestic servant. Anyway, we couldn't afford him now.

There were many other things that we could not afford now—and all because of that one fateful day that month. We could not afford our home, our car, and our way of life as we knew it. It was a month of loss. Shammi and I lost our father; Mummy lost her husband; my grandmother in Bangalore lost another son; my grandmother in Bombay lost a son-in-law; my aunts and uncles lost a brother; CPT lost an able employee; and Thambi lost his job.

My life now mimics that of my parents. When I visit home, I say I live in Washington DC, but not quite as I live in Fairfax, Virginia. Anil and I have three boys, no girls. "Just think," Anil told me when the twins were born, "You will have four grown men looking after you soon." When I think of my boys all grown up, I know how my father felt then when he told my mother how much he was looking forward to the attention from his grown daughters. Even though I secretly longed for a girl, Anil is content with his brood of boys. "No point wanting something that we have no control over," he says.

I did not know then how much I would miss my father. The changes were all so exciting that I got caught up in them. But in the years to come, just watching a "whole" family driving by would make me feel sad. Even now, whenever Anil and I and our boys drive out of our garage together, or I think of Shammi driving around Chennai with her husband and two girls, my sense of happiness is mingled with a sadness for what we did not have as children. I use "whole" in the strictest sense of the word. According to all those family planning billboards, a family had to have a mother, a father, and children. Now, we could never be that. We were a family still, but not whole. At thirty-one, my mother was widowed, and the older I got, the more sadness I felt for all the time she missed out on with my father, who was thirty-nine when he died. Her social life as she had known it with Daddy was gone now. They had enjoyed going to dinner parties or an occasional cocktail party or two together, and now in Jaipur, we had none of that. Where couples were invited, she was not.

Daddy would have loved his grandchildren—girls or boys. If I pause for a moment, I can remember, even now after more than thirty years, how he smelled as I bent over him that day in the hospital. Some moments from those distraught times are branded forever in my memory. I shall always remember my Gopal Uncle bending over my father's body. Sixteen years after my father's death, this uncle would die, leaving my oldest uncle to grieve alone for his lost brothers. There were four in all, and each one of them was close to the other. At family gatherings, I remember them joking and teasing each other and in general having a good time. I see old black and white photographs of the family, and I see my father's boyish figure sitting with all his nieces and nephews, becoming one of them. He looks so young that it is hard to believe he is their uncle. It is hard to believe he is now dead.

Thirty-eight years is a long time to remember something so vividly, but I do. Whenever I have had the misfortune to attend another Hindu funeral, the day of my father's funeral comes back to me. Somehow, of the ten years that I spent with him, that day has stayed the most vivid in my mind—the climax of our short life together. In my own married life, I had to cross the milestones that I had made up for myself mentally, without telling a soul. First, Anil and I had to cross our eleventh wedding anniversary, an anniversary my mother never celebrated. Daddy died four months short of theirs. Then Akshay, our oldest, had to have his tenth birthday. Daddy died two months short of mine. It is as if I am living a life parallel to that of my mother's.

Soon after my father's death, somebody told my mother that Daddy should not have used the *Bullworker* without consulting a doctor first. For a while after that, I remember my mother wondering often if Daddy would have still been with us if he hadn't used that device. The *Bullworker* became the proverbial unwanted stepchild in our family, and none of us mentioned it. Did all that pulling and straining damage his heart muscles? I am obsessed with my own weight these days and exercise regularly even though Anil tells me I look fine. "Exercising at my age is more for my health than any other reason," I argue with him. "It is more for blood sugar, cholesterol, and blood pressure than for the figure." The heart attack that robbed Daddy of the rest of his life has made me paranoid about my health and the health of my family. Meanwhile, the hypochondriac me peeps out once in a while, which displeases me.

Goodbye Bombay

My father died on 19th of May, and by the end of June we were in a train heading for Jaipur. It had been a hectic past month, with an endless stream of relatives visiting, helping, and deciding what was the best thing for my mother to do next. In just over one month we had packed, given away, or sold all our worldly possessions. My sister does not remember much of that strange month, but I can replay everything in my mind like a broken record. Why doesn't the record shatter, completely erasing all memory of that awful month?

Why do I remember so much?

Staying on in Bombay without Daddy was out of question. It was too big a city for so young a family. Despite Mummy's newly acquired teaching job, we could not stay on. The natural choice then, would have been for us to move to Bangalore as we "belonged" to that place, but Mummy was adamant. She refused to live in a place where nosy distant relatives would raise a finger at every move she made as a young widow. She wanted to raise her two girls as she saw fit, and not as they thought she should. So she chose Jaipur instead, where her older sister and brother-in-law were doctors, and nobody knew her.

When we left for Jaipur, we left all our furniture behind. In the living room, there was that comfortable *divan*, a settee, always covered by a beautiful spread that Mummy would change from time to time. The latest was a hand-woven piece from our visit to the northeastern state of Assam where we had gone to visit Daddy's sister, my Vimmu Aunty, in Shillong. Just the previous year, Daddy had ordered two chairs with slightly reclining backs and arm rests, and with cushions thrown on these chairs and on the *divan*, our living room had become a comfortable and lovely place to sit. To the left of this room was a split bamboo shelf that Daddy had proudly designed himself. The shelf turned away from the living room into a tiny groove in the room, and held his cache of liquor bottles that he called "his bar." Mummy had added her touch to this bar by placing a huge glass bowl with a money plant in it that soon grew and cascaded down the shelf on the living room side adding some greenery to the room.

When we had left Pinjore to come to Bombay four years earlier, I was too young to remember the details of that house. The Bombay apartment was the first "home" for me, and I loved it. I liked the way Mummy arranged the living room—not expensively, but very tastefully.

I did not much care for the bed that Shammi and I shared in our Bombay apartment, but Mummy and Daddy's bedroom set was new and very elegant. It was not a big bed—made to order to fit their room—and there was a matching dressing table with a tall mirror that Mummy could stand in front of and see her entire self while she draped her sari. Just on Sunday mornings, this room became our room too; Shammi's and mine, as we cuddled up to Daddy, one on either side, while Mummy was busy preparing a Sunday brunch in the kitchen. Who would sleep on Daddy's right and who would be on his left was cause enough for a big fight every Sunday. Both Shammi and I wanted his right side. Once we were settled, we took possession of that side of his face, his hair, and that hand. Shammi would comb her side of his hair, and I would do what I wanted with my side, so that Daddy ended up with a different look on each side. It was as if he ended up with two different personalities once we were through with him. Often, if he hadn't had a haircut in a while, he would end up with a tiny ponytail standing straight on his head. Daddy of course enjoyed all this, and did not complain at all.

The dining room furniture in our Bombay apartment was the only set that had been made to order in Pinjore. It was made for our family—just four chairs. When we ultimately moved into a house by ourselves in Jaipur—Mummy, Shammi, and I—all this furniture appeared as if by magic, giving us the much needed security and familiarity.

Whilst the whole world's attention was riveted on the Vietnam War, I was a chubby ten-year-old, waging my own personal war against fat. Any doctor would have declared at a glance that my skeletal age was way ahead of my biological age; I was a big ten-year-old. Even though the glamour-studded Bombay film world then was filled with heroines with big chests and even larger bottoms, Mummy did not think that I was growing up right. She at once put me on a sugar-free diet, hoping to get rid of the folds of fat on my chest and abdomen. All the elders in the family promptly criticized this action, but she held her ground. No daughter of hers was growing up fat. Being big had advantages, however. I was unanimously chosen the leader in charge of the group of kids who had to walk to the bus stop a little away from home. Their fathers, like Daddy had, worked at CPT, on the main road in Mulund at the very end of Bombay that went on into Thana district.

Shammi and I were a white-collared engineer's children, while the other children were the offspring of blue-collared factory workers. Professional hierarchy at work trickled down to our living conditions too, and the residential colony behind the factory consisted of two buildings. We lived in the one that had only two large apartments on each floor. The other building was a *chawl*, with tiny one- or two-room units with common baths at both ends of each floor. While the apartments in our building each had a balcony of its own, the *chawl* had a long common corridor outside the units, where people could sit to get some fresh air.

This distinction in residential allotment ended, however, on the playground. There was one set of swings, one seesaw, and one slide. We played together and had fun together. My best friend at that time was Sheila Poyail, whose mother made the best mutton-stew in the typical Kerala style, and she let me have some with steaming white rice whenever I visited. I often think of Sheila now. She is my age, and I am sure has a husband and children of her own. Every morning, I would lead a bunch of kids from the colony down the dusty side road to the main road and wait for the school bus to take us to Holy Cross Convent. I had to first look left, then look right, and then give the go ahead to the others to cross the street. In our white shirts and red and white-checkered pinafores and heavy book-bags on our backs, we looked like a flock of geese waddling across the street to the bus stop on the other side.

I see the bus now in the distance, and tell the other kids. As soon as the bus stops, there is a rush to get in. I am the last. I climb up the steps looking down at the floor, not daring to look up. I can see her pointed red shoes with the high heels. I can also see her shapely crossed legs as she sits in the first row of the bus. The kids are not settling down fast enough, and I have to wait my turn. I am impatient. I look up and see Mrs. Pareira, a teacher who also rides the bus, looking at me with a big grin on her beautiful face. Her teeth shine brightly against her painted red lips. Her hair is up in a fashionable roll, and her dress clings to her shapely body. She is an Anglo-Indian, and looks great in her frocks. As soon as I see her, she reaches over to pinch my cheek, saying heartily, "Hello Fatty!"

I sensed the special affection Mrs. Pareira had for me. I realized that she pinched my cheeks because she found them irresistible. Her wide grin and the twinkle in her eyes were reserved just for me as she greeted me on the bus.

I do not remember saying goodbye to anyone when we left Bombay. Journeys, especially long ones, have always excited me, and this one was no different. I often wonder now what has happened to all the faces that stare back at me when I look at class photographs taken at the Holy Cross Convent. With one face I remember the name, with another I remember a birthday party, and with another a fight that I had. My fourth grade teacher, Mrs. Badrunisa Sheikh, sits amongst us with a big tummy, as she was just about to go on maternity leave. Did she have a girl? A boy? An adult now, no doubt.

She drifts in silently, watching, waiting—the emptiness is a barrier. Only the dried split bamboo-shoot shelf remains, a testament to lifelessness. The money plant sprouts afresh and cascades down; life goes on. Mementoes from a bygone life remain on the walls; a trip taken, a wedding attended, a mask—so she looks up. The silence is a bit loud, and even the tiny creak of the door makes a jarring sound. Gigantic ice slabs that do not melt have a cooling effect, and she watches and waits. And then he is carried in, his lifeless body covered with white and placed on the ice, away from the sultry heat of the outside. "Won't the ice hurt him?" she wonders.

I do not remember the other rooms in the apartment as vividly as I do that living room. But I do remember the balcony, because it was from there that I saw Daddy for the last time. I remember his bed, because Shammi and I lay on it with him every Sunday morning, playing with his hair. Akshay is too old to cuddle up to us now, but Aditya and Anurag, the twins, still do. They lie on either side of Anil and insist on his playing guessing games with them. I look at Anil's balding head and think of Daddy's thick and full head of hair. No opportunity for play on this head, I chuckle to myself, but then these are boys, and unlike girls, they are not interested in hairdressing.

To this day, I cannot explain Mrs. Pareira's fascination with my cheeks, or her consistency in pinching them day in and day out. I hated it, and I can still feel the pinch. Being called Fatty hurt less than the physical pain of a cheek that had been pinched. And because the pain of a pinched cheek has stayed on in memory, I have always been extremely gentle with similarly enticing cheeks. I run my fingers on them lightly, or at the most give them a light kiss. I never pinch. Even though I loved the way Mrs. Pareira looked, I dreaded looking at her, dearly wishing she wouldn't hurt me so. She was everything I was not at that time. She was tall and thin with great legs. Her skin was smooth, an even brown, and her neatly coffered jet-black hair was a striking contrast. She always wore shoes that matched her dress, as did her lipstick, and her smile was dazzling. And of course to top it all, I happened to see her husband once at a school function, and he was a hunk straight out of a Mills & Boon Romance. I saw Mrs. Pareira for the last time when she visited our house a few days after Daddy died. I can see her even now, sitting on the living room divan talking softly with Mummy. Not once during that visit did she pinch my cheeks.

The First Year

When a sand storm—*Aandhi*—is brewing, the sky turns a deep brownish-red. The wind picks up, and everyone hurries to close windows and doors. To be caught outside during the storm means that your eyes, nose, mouth, ears, and hair, will be full of sand. Millions of tiny sand particles slap your face, and it stings. Even with closed doors and windows, once the storm has passed, you have to sweep the house and dust all the furniture. Just after we moved to Jaipur after losing Daddy and before schools reopened after the break, Shammi and I, and Sanju and Jaideep, our cousins, were always out in the yard, playing. Apart from lunch and snack breaks, and hurried visits to the toilet, only the threat of an *Aandhi* forced us inside during the day. So I was terribly excited that day in June, when Jayu Aunty, my mother's older sister with whom we stayed for that first year in Jaipur, shouted for us to come in—I had heard of sand storms, and now I would experience one.

We ran in, the four of us, and I went to our room to tell my mother all about it. I found her sitting on the bed, saying and doing nothing. She stared at the wall opposite her with tears streaking down her cheeks, as if in a trance. Her *mangalsutra*, the thick gold chain she always wore around her neck, was now thrown on the bed next to her. The gold bangles from her wrists were there too, and she no longer wore the big, round, red *bindi* on her forehead. Amma was sitting in front of her wringing her hands and feeling helpless. Biri Aunty, my aunt's friend, was visiting, and taking her slippers off at the door, she gingerly approached Mummy's bed and sat next to her. She too said nothing. I did not go near Mummy, as I did not know what to do or what to say. It was scary to see my mother in this state.

When she becomes a widow, a Hindu woman loses the right to wear the sacred *mangalsutra*, the chain around her neck that her husband has tied during their wedding. She cannot wear red glass bangles on her wrists, nor can she wear the red *sindoor* in the parting of her hair or the red *bindi* on her forehead. My family was too progressive to object to anything my mother did, but on her own she decided to wear a black *bindi* instead of a red one, and that day in Jaipur, she removed her *mangalsutra*, and I haven't seen it since. Did she have all the gold in it melted to make some other jewelry for us? Does she still have it? She decided that she would not wear lipstick any more, the only make-up that she had truly loved. From color, she went to black and white.

Mummy had never been an overly devout person, yet she had celebrated all festivals religiously and followed all customs and traditions that she had learnt from her mother. My grandparents were wealthy, and the advent of each religious festival was a time for lavish preparation and celebration. My grandfather loved to see his wife and daughters decked in jewelry and good clothes, and he indulged their every whim. Mummy had always been a good dresser—she took care, and it showed. In her childhood it was her father, and in marriage it was Daddy who indulged and adored her, and as a family we did not bow too much to tradition and superstition. But, we prayed regularly. Now with Daddy's death, however, Mummy renounced God. Despite doing every thing right, things had gone terribly wrong, and she was angry with Him. As a child, I sensed Mummy's anger, but I did not understand it. It was anger that made her strong; it was anger that made her willful; and it was anger that made her want to move on with her life and not dwell in the past; a past in which she had lost her husband, and had to give up her house and a way of life that was steadily moving upwards on the luxury scale.

Daddy's heart attack had not only deprived him of life, it had attacked his family too. It had attacked on the sly, and it had won. Mummy, Shammi, and I had to humbly retreat in defeat.

Every day, Mummy wrote something in a notebook. She spent a long time bent over it, and sometimes she cried as she wrote. When she was done, she put the notebook away so I could not peek inside. One day, she sat next to me with the notebook and pen in her hand.

"Do you want to see what I write in here Suppy?" She asked. I just nodded.

It was lined; a child's schoolbook, but Mummy ignored the lines. She started at the very top and filled the entire page in her neat handwriting. And all she wrote over and over and over again, page after page was:

Satyan Satyan Satyan Satyan Satyan Satyan Satyan Satyan Satyan Satyan...

"He is my God Suppy," she told me. "I do not want to forget him."

Instead of the *Vishnu Sahasranam* Mummy chanted Daddy's name.

Shammi and I could not comfort her. We did not know how. We never sat by her talking about Daddy. In my ten-year-old mind was the firm conviction that talking about him would bring her more grief, so I took the easy way out—I did not mention him.

Sanju and Jaideep had become more like brothers as we lived together for that first year after our move to Jaipur. Their friends were our friends, and we played together, ate together, and fought together. When we fought, we ganged up—us sisters against those two brothers. Sanju was seven, almost a year older than Shammi, and Jaideep was four, the baby of the family. At ten, I was the oldest and held a position of authority. Pramod Uncle's parents visited often and became our surrogate grandparents. We called them Bauaa and Babaji just like Sanju and Jaideep did. Babaji read most of the time and kept to himself. Bauaa was short, and even at ten I towered over her, but her well-rounded body gave her personality. Her hair was completely gray, which she wore in a long braid, and her perfect dentures were a sharp contrast to her sagging wrinkle-riddled cheeks. Her visits meant that we could have the tasty *Prashad* she made to offer the Gods. Every time she did her special *puja*, I would be ready with a small bowl and spoon to have this offering to the Gods, which was made simply from whole-wheat flour and sugar and a little cardamom powder. Bauaa liked Mummy and she showed it.

"I like you Tara," she used to say to Mummy again and again. "You are very nice."

From Holy Cross in Bombay to St. Angela Sophia in Jaipur, school was not so much of a change for us—both convents, both run by Catholic Nuns; only a change in uniform. Sister Theodora, the Principal of St. Angela Sophia School, was a big woman with a large chest and a loud voice. Her gait was manly, and she ordered the peons around constantly. The Mother Superior, on the other hand, was a much shorter, rounder, and gentler person. They were very kind to Mummy, and served us tea and biscuits when Mummy took us to visit them the first time.

"It is all God's will Mrs. Satyan," they said sympathetically. "We are here for you. We will help you." It was very exciting for Shammi and me—we had new school uniforms and new books and a new book bag. We passed the entrance test for the school, and Shammi would be in the 1st grade and I would be in the 5th grade, and best of all, Mummy would be teaching there too. The Nuns wanted her to.

It was nice to have Mummy with us at school. She was the homeroom teacher of another section of the 5th grade, and I would often bump into her in the corridors. Going to school with her and eating lunch with her and coming back home with her became our routine. At night we slept together on the same bed with Mummy in the middle—both Shammi and I wanted her. It gave us much-needed security, and having us close to her gave her comfort to heal the wound in her heart.

Living together for one whole year took a lot of effort on all our parts. It was easy to like my uncle. He was patient, gentle, sweet, and loving. And he always smiled. He loved children, and never shouted at Sanju and Jaideep or at Shammi and me. Mummy and Jayu Aunty had their differences, but that did not stop us from loving her unconditionally. Pramod Uncle and Jayu Aunty had opened their hearts and home to us for one whole year, and Mummy never let Shammi and me forget that.

Once, on the way to school, Mummy cried softly.

"Let's run away Suppy," she said. "And not come back here, ever."

"No Mummy No! We cannot do that." I was terrified when she talked like that.

Shammi kept quiet; she was too young.

"Blood is thicker than water," Mummy said later, and still does.

In the winter of that very same year, we were distracted from the turmoil in our lives by India's war with neighboring Pakistan. The radio was always on in the house as Pramod Uncle loved to listen to music all the time, but during the war we needed it to keep us informed about what was going on as regular news bulletins interrupted everything. And then there were patriotic songs to encourage our *Jawaans*, our soldiers. On the rare occasion that there was no news of war, we could hear film songs again.

Even though we had no family member in the Army, war was scary. The siren we heard every evening heralding curfew was scarier. It started out in a low moan and kept getting louder, ultimately reaching a crescendo before waning off. Everyone said Jaipur was in danger because it was so close to the Pakistan border. In Jodhpur, which was even closer to the border than Jaipur, bombs actually fell.

We had moved into another house just before the war started, and I felt more secure here. It had more rooms, and Mummy, Shammi, and I could have our own room without displacing Jayu Aunty and Pramod Uncle from theirs. Their family had the front part of the house, while we had the back. During the threat of air raids, we had blackouts and could not turn our lights on after dark. All windowpanes had to have brown paper glued on them so even the candlelight would not filter out. It was thrilling to do our homework in dim lights, huddled in comforters, as the winters in Jaipur were bitterly cold. Often, during blackouts, we heard airplanes flying above us, and as we had no way of knowing whether they were ours or the enemy's, we always imagined the worst and held our breaths till they passed.

In school, we had bomb drills. A loud electric buzzer would go off through the entire school, and we had to drop whatever we had been doing and take shelter under the desks. We were taught to crouch low, with our palms covering both our ears and faces to the floor, the theory being that in case of an air attack, if the roof caved in, our desks would break the fall and protect us; a little bit at least.

The only part about the bitter winter that I disliked was getting up very early to go to school. We were in the first shift of the school bus, so we had to leave home at 5:30 a.m. even though school started at 9:00. Mummy bundled us up in layers of clothes to keep us warm. Both Shammi and I wore an undershirt and a sleeveless woolen sweater over that to keep our chests warm. Then came the sky blue uniform shirt and the dark blue pleated skirt, with the red school tie. We then wore a red sleeveless sweater with a V-neck, and finally a red long-sleeved cardigan. If Mummy thought that it was still too cold for us, we wore the red school blazer with the school's emblem to top everything off and a scarf over our heads to cover our ears. To keep our legs warm, we wore red stockings, and of course black leather shoes. Much to our delight, we got to bathe every other day in the winter. Taking our clothes off inside the cold bathroom was supreme torture, even though the water we bathed in was steaming hot. Once we reached school, Mummy made us do extra work while she did her corrections. After school, we were the first ones home; the children in the second shift waited at school and reached home later.

In one year, Mummy transformed herself from a housewife, to a working woman in charge of her family. In one year, we left behind the bad *Bombayya Hindi* and learnt to speak "proper Hindi." In one year, we were ready to move out on our own and make Jaipur our permanent home. Mummy liked it here, as the people were friendly and helpful. So we looked for and found a house that had a "to-let" board on it. It was close to Jayu Aunty's house and Pramod Uncle knew the owner, who agreed to rent it out to us. Mummy also decided that she wanted to be her own boss, and started a tiny nursery school in the large house we had rented. This way she would be home all the time for us. We just needed the kitchen and two of the rooms for ourselves—one as a dining room and the other as our bedroom. Our living room doubled as her office during the day. Every year, she decided, she would add one more grade to the school and make it bigger. When the Mulund Chapter of the Rotary Club of Bombay came to know of the school, they gifted all the Montessori equipment for the nursery class—their way of honoring Daddy, who had been an active member for the last four years of his life. Today, thirty-nine years later, Blue Bells is a fully accredited High School with a separate building of its own and Mummy serving as its Director.

It was after we moved that I saw the pieces of furniture that had belonged to us in Bombay. Where had they been stored? I never bothered to ask, but now they appeared magically. The bamboo shelf that Daddy had made into a bar was there—we used it as a bookshelf now. The low divan that I so loved was there too. Just before he died, Daddy had gone to the studio for a black and white passport photograph—maybe for an I.D. Mummy had that photograph enlarged and framed, and it hung prominently in our living room. Soon we had a semblance of our old house back. We had Daddy back too, to look up to and pray to and remember.

Mummy continued to grieve for Daddy privately in those first years after we moved to Jaipur, and on occasion this grief would become more visible when the invisible shield that she had erected around her would crack and we would get a glimpse of a broken woman mourning her loss. It would be comforting then, to be physically close to her—our way of comforting her. Shammi and I missed cuddling up to Daddy on Sunday mornings, and could not smell him on our pillows in Jaipur, and that made us want to be as close to Mummy as possible all the time.

It is almost forty years now since my father's death, but I have not had the courage to discuss the grief that Mummy felt with her. My parents were together for less than eleven years; I have been with Anil for more than double those years and look forward to many many more—there is so much that she missed, but I cannot tell her that.

"You know Suppy, Daddy is a wonderful dream of my past," she tells me now. The last thirty odd years have hardened my mother. She has become independent to the extent of becoming stubborn, and rightfully so. In a so-called "man's" world, she had to become like that to survive. And that determination to fend for one's own self rubbed off on her girls too.

My children call my father *Nana*, the Hindi term for a maternal grandfather, when they look at a picture of his, and the word Nana comes more easily to my lips than Daddy. I did not mention our father while we were growing up for fear of hurting my mother, and she did not mention him for fear of hurting us and making our loss more obvious. Shammi does not like that. She feels that talking about him would have kept the memories alive for her. But then, memories have a way of fading away no matter what.

Even though I was almost ten when Daddy died, I find that I have to make an effort to remember him now.

Snapshots

The only photograph of Daddy that hung in our house in Jaipur was that enlarged version of a black and white picture. For Mummy, Shammi, and me, he would forever be like that—black, wavy hair, with not even a hint of gray in it, which had been combed back from the forehead, a straight moustache that lined his upper lip, and thick eyebrows that met at the center of his face, just above the nose. The hair in the bridge above the nose was very sparse, and one had to look closely at his photograph to see that it was actually a continuation of the eyebrows. The right eyebrow on the far side, away from the nose, had a fork in it in the end. A childhood injury, maybe, that had killed off the hair follicles in that area. It was a handsome face, and whenever I look at the picture, I feel he is looking straight at me. I have often wondered about how he would have aged. Would he have lost any of that hair on his head? Would he have become thinner and shrunk in height? Or would he be one of those who age gracefully and seem forever young? Anyway, fate had seen to it that my father would always be thirty-nine years old. Sometime during the first few years after Daddy's death, my mother channeled her grief into creating an album full of his pictures. Shammi and I do not remember seeing her do this. When we were at school perhaps? Or was it quietly at night after we had gone to bed? Neither did she talk about her project nor did she show anyone this album after it was completed. Well into my teenage years, I found this picture album tucked in amidst Daddy's clothes in the chocolate brown Godrej Almirah in our bedroom. In those beginning years after moving to Jaipur, we had acquired two more generic brand steel cupboards that were a light steel gray in color, but Daddy's clothes were kept in the "Godrej." The album was big with a golden brown cover and tassels that held the black pages together. I had opened the Almirah to put something back in one of the lower shelves, and I saw the spine of the album sticking out a little in between Daddy's plastic wrapped shirts.

"You can look through the album Suppy," Mummy had said when I asked her about it. "But please be careful." A thin page made of white tissue paper that had a self-design on it separated each page of the album so the photographs would not rub against each other. When I looked to the left page, I had a sneak preview of the right page through this semi-transparent tissue. I was careful not to open the album too wide, treating it reverently, like a holy book.

The inside of the cover of the album was covered with pieces of paper of all sizes and shades of white with Daddy's signature on it. Mummy had cut these out from wherever she could find them. On official papers, letters, notebooks, book jackets—even signatures doodled on scrap paper, just testing a pen. There was one piece of paper with all our names written in his hand too—his family, his girls. In that list, his children were "Supriya" and "Sharmila" and not Suppy and Shammi. As always, Mummy was "Tara," too small a name to be shortened any further. Daddy wrote the "S" in his name in a funny way. It was almost a semi-circle facing the left. The rest of the letters written at an angle followed this, and a single line at the bottom finished the signature with a flourish. He signed himself simply as "Satyan." No more. He reserved this strangely written "S" just for his signature, however. He did not write the "S" in Shammi's and my name in the same style. I compared each signature to the others. Except for a change in ink color, they were identical. The same oddly shaped "S" and the same angle. I could imagine Mummy lovingly running her fingers over his name.

Daddy was the youngest son in a large family. There was one older sister and three older brothers and three sisters after him— eight living of all the children my grandmother bore. There were others who died in infancy or perished in her womb. The family lost track, and it does not matter. If I close my eyes now, I can picture myself leafing through that album all over again.

Facing the signature page, is a family portrait of his family, and I look at it eagerly to see where Daddy is. The photograph is in black and white with a hint of brown to it as if the studio had tried to develop it in a slight sepia tone. Sitting on high back chairs to the right of the group are my paternal grandparents. A regal turban covers my grandfather's head. He is dressed very formally in a coat and tie, and strangely enough, the turban on his head and the vermilion line running the length of his forehead, from his nose to where his hair starts—the *Shricharanu* that all followers of Vishnu applied after finishing their bath and daily prayers—does not look out of place with his very western attire. I look at my grandfather for a while and decide that Daddy had his lips. My grandmother wears the traditional nine-yard silk sari that all South-Indian women wore. A different version is worn today, and the sari is only six yards long now. To the left of the group, in two similar chairs, sit my oldest aunt and her husband. Standing next to that aunt is her daughter, my father's oldest niece, who is perhaps three or four in that picture. In a similar pose, next to my grandmother, is another of my aunts, and she is the same age as her own niece. Mother and daughter had given birth at the same time.

The other children stand or sit all around looking straight at the camera. Daddy is on the floor, just in front of his oldest sister and brother-in-law. I recognize him because of his eyebrows. He wears baggy knickers and a shirt and his arms encircle his half-raised knees. I try to guess his age. Ten? Twelve? The eyes that look at the camera in that picture have the same glint that the one that is hanging in our home now has. I count all my aunts and uncles and find one missing—the youngest one. She is in your grandmother's tummy, Mummy explains when I ask her.

"How strange," I wonder aloud, "to be younger than your own niece."

There are no more photographs of Daddy as a boy. On the very next page he was a young man, tall and lanky, with a thin moustache and wavy hair that looks wet and is parted to one side. Mummy had grouped the photographs well. I look closely at one of them where he is in his cricket gear. He holds the bat in his hand and looks up into the camera. His mouth seems almost too wide for his slim face, and I decide that I prefer the face I now remember. His face had widened in adulthood, and his mouth seemed more proportionate. I try to imagine his life at the age he is in the cricket picture. My grandfather had died young, and Daddy and his siblings grew up without a father just as Shammi and I were doing.

I am not interested in any of the photographs of Daddy's youth. He looks different and so do my aunts and uncles. They seem simple back then. Even their way of dressing is awkward and not sophisticated. They have all grown up to become successful people with nice families of their own, but here they seem devoid of color— yes! That's it. All these black and white pictures prevent them from coming to life.

As for Daddy, I did not know him then, so I am not interested. I have to keep his memory alive, and I want to remember him as he was just before he died. Not his younger version. In the photographs where he stands with groups—his college friends—I have to peer to make out where he is. All the men dress alike, and all of their hairstyles are similar. None of the men wore t-shirts when Daddy was a young man. The shirts are half-sleeved or full depending on the weather. And all of them wear under shirts, the round neck of which can be seen as the collar button of the shirt and also the one below is always open.

I quickly flip through some more pages until at last I come to a big photograph, the same size as the album page, of my parents' wedding. The bride and the groom are sitting down for this one, and she is to his left. It is a close up, and even though this one is also a black and white, I can see all the details of Mummy's sari and the jewelry she wore on her big day.

There is not much make-up on Mummy's face. I cannot make out if her lips are covered with a light colored lipstick or if there is just some gloss. There is kohl in her eyes, and the *bindi* on her forehead looks black and is vertical—not the usual red and round one. It was the fashion to wear it like that in the late 1950s and early '60s. Film stars wore it like that, and they wore their blouses tight and with long sleeves. A diaphanous sari covered their chest through which everyone could see their pointed breasts, but Mummy does not do that. She does wear the sleeves of her silk blouse long, and they come up to her elbows, but she wears a heavy silk sari, and nothing shows through that. I cannot tell what color the sari is, but I know the jewelry well, and I feel connected to the picture.

Daddy wears a dark suit and tie, and his face has already filled out from the earlier photographs. Both of them have fresh flower garlands around their necks—chrysanthemums, of different colors perhaps to give the garlands a pattern, with gold and silver thread here and there to give it a glitter. They look straight at the camera, and I can hear the many instructions from the elders and the photographer about how to sit and where to look.

I was born a few days short of ten months from the day of my parents' wedding, and it is comforting to know, looking at the picture, that soon they will have me and I shall be a part of them.

Halfway through my trip through the pages of the album, Shammi joined me, wanting to look at the photographs too, but I impatiently shooed her off. I wanted to be lost in that world alone, and no one could disturb that. It was a lazy Sunday afternoon, and Mummy was busy in the kitchen and left me alone too.

I continued browsing through Daddy's life, and soon found that I was looking at pictures of myself as a baby. Because it was an album dedicated to Daddy, all the photographs had him in them. The only photographs I saw now were the ones in which he carries me or is sitting or standing next to me. I stop for a long time at one in which I am about two years old. He is carrying me, my small arms tight around his neck, my face touching his. Both of us look at the camera—it has to be Mummy taking the picture, calling out to me to look at her perhaps.

Daddy is in his under shirt, one of those that have no sleeves. The top of his trousers show just a tiny bit in the photograph. I see his big muscular upper arms, his closely cropped hair, and the strong hands as they encircle me. When he smiled slightly, only one half of his mouth stretched, and it reminds me now of Clark Gable smiling at Scarlet O'Hara in *Gone With the Wind*. It must have been summer then, with just the three of us at home as I am just in my underwear and an undershirt we called a petticoat. These petticoats could be pleated like frocks or straight like t-shirts, and they were always made of white cotton cloth. In the picture, I wear the straight one.

There are many more pictures of Daddy. Daddy in Germany, Daddy at Trafalgar Square in London with a pigeon perched on his left shoulder, Daddy at work—testimonies to his life that I had heard about from Mummy. In the later pages, I re-live the vacations we took as a family as I re-visit the hill station, Matheran, or the state of Assam. And then at the very end of the album, I finally come to a life that I knew and remembered—the last four years of Daddy's life that we spent in Bombay. Ironically, the Bombay photographs are in color, proof that those are the most vivid of my memories and they shall always remain so.

I ended my journey by lingering for the longest time on those last pictures. Mummy had done something wonderful to keep his memory alive, and Daddy is at his most handsome self in these later photographs. I could see the color of his eyes, the shade of his skin, and his charming smile that made the photograph come to life. On the very last page of the album was a photograph of Mummy and Daddy—a formal portrait taken in a studio just before he left us. Daddy looks dashing in a rust colored shirt; Mummy is elegantly draped in a pink and black silk sari and looks beautiful. Both look happy, and rust is my favorite color.

Tara

I have tried very hard to erase that memory of my mother from my mind, but it refuses to go away. The haunting of this memory continues periodically, and I have to physically shake my head to be rid of it. I do not want to give in to the gloom this memory causes, for then it will become a chain of memories that will cling to my mind like a leech. I do not want to see her like that, standing at the top of the stairs in that big hospital in Bombay, tears streaming down her cheeks, her arms outstretched, waiting to gather Shammi and me in her embrace. Even at that moment I did not realize what had gone wrong. I knew my father had been taken to the hospital the previous evening, but did not know that he had died. He had left behind him a broken woman, but by no means a weak woman.

Mummy was four months short of her thirty-second birthday and eleventh wedding anniversary on that miserable day in May. Because it was a lazy month with schools closed for the summer break, it was a time when either we visited relatives or had someone visiting us. Daddy's death changed this month from a lazy one to one that was filled with grief and remembrance. May is a reminder of what I lost, what my mother lost, what my family lost, and most of all, what my father lost. He had missed growing old with the woman he loved; he had missed seeing his two girls grow up into adults.

Up until then, September had always been a mixed month for celebrating and remembering for my mother. Her birthday was in September, and so was my father's. September was also when she married Daddy in 1960. But, it was also in September that she lost her father, just twenty-one days before her wedding. Invitations had gone out, the marriage hall booked, the wedding saris and jewelry bought, and she was busy with more shopping with her mother and sisters in Bangalore when the telegram arrived saying that my grandfather had died of a massive coronary thrombosis in their home town of Warangal in the southern state of Andhra Pradesh. Just the day before, Feroze Gandhi, Indira Gandhi's estranged husband, had died of the same type of heart attack, and this became my grandfather's parting claim to fame.

As a child, I felt very important saying those two big words—coronary thrombosis—I just liked the way they sounded, and I would tell my friends with morbid pride that what killed Feroze Gandhi killed my grandfather too. In comparison, my father had died of an ordinary heart attack, which had no fancy medical name attached to it.

Mummy inherited her father's big structure, and when I see old black and white photographs, I see the resemblance between them. The lips are the same and so is the shape of their faces. NC, as his family and friends affectionately called my grandfather, was dark in complexion, while Amma was petite and light-skinned.

I remember visiting that big house in Warangal, where my mother grew up, as a young girl during one summer break from school. The street outside had become a busy thoroughfare as the town had expanded in the years after NC's death. The house was a big white structure with its main entrance to the side. I could picture my grandfather returning home in his tonga after a full day of treating patients at his office in the Azam Jahi Cloth Mills where he was the mill doctor. Servants had to run up the driveway to open the gates and let the horse drawn carriage in. NC loved his horse, and after getting down from the tonga, he never failed to pat the horse on its neck before going into the house. After unharnessing the horse from the carriage, the servant led it to the back of the house where it would join the family cow for an evening of leisure and rest. Soon after NC's death, the horse was sold to a man on the other side of the town. The very next day, the man came to my grandparents' house in a panic saying that the horse had disappeared. The horse had walked across town and stood patiently outside the gate to my grandparents' house, waiting to be let in.

Mummy remembers her father looking down into his left palm periodically and shaking his head and making clicking sounds with his tongue.

"Not a long life," he muttered to himself often. I have always wondered why a man of precise science will give in to the unpredictability of palmistry and start believing in it. It is almost as if his belief willed the unthinkable to happen. When ultimately the end came, NC had no family with him. With him was his dear friend, Dakshinamurthy, a renowned palmist who later told the family, "There was no line for *kanyadaan*, in NC's palms." He was not destined to give away a daughter's hand in marriage. After his death, several Brahmin pundits were consulted who told Amma that according to Hindu beliefs, the very act of giving away a daughter in marriage, the *kanyaadan*, was good for the departed soul and would help its passage into the afterlife. So, the wedding took place as planned.

Because NC believed that he was not going to live long, he had insisted that Mummy get married soon. His older daughter was a doctor, and he knew she would be OK. His youngest had decided whom she would marry, and he was content on that score. Besides his looks, Mummy had inherited her father's stubborn nature, and had insisted on going to medical school. NC had never made any distinctions between his sons and daughters. They had to be educated, they could have friends both male and female, they could eat mutton in their Muslim and Christian friends' houses, and they

49

did not have to learn how to cook. But when it came to Mummy attending medical school, he put his foot down.

"Please listen to me Taramma, I shall buy you nice diamond earrings," he pleaded affectionately, addressing her with mock respect, and Mummy gave in. Just as she gave in when she had wanted to play badminton in college and could not because her father did not let her wear the *salwar kameez*.

"Only Muslim girls wear that," he declared, "and no daughter of mine shall."

"But how can I play badminton in this long skirt?" Mummy had argued. It was of no use, and she had to give up playing that game. He was very progressive in most matters, she told me, but there were a couple of times when he did not relent.

And now he convinced her to marry and chose for her a life partner who was an engineer in the dacoit infested Chambal Valley in northern India. His mother had come home to see Mummy, and agreed to have NC's second daughter as her daughter-in-law. After all, the girl came from a wealthy family, she thought, and promptly handed my grandfather a list things she expected him to provide my mother with.

Both Shammi and I loved to hear the story of what happened next. "Maybe you would have been a boy," I would tease Shammi and also add, "It would have been nice to have a brother."

"Maybe I would be the older sister," Shammi would retort.

Mummy had disliked her future mother-in-law the instant she laid eyes on her, and had revolted to the fact that the woman had demanded things from her father. In Iyengar families there is no system of dowry, and because he had given in to the demands of this mean woman, she had scolded her father.

"How can I marry a man with a mother like this? I have not even seen him." She could be adamant too, and her father knew it. An elderly cousin came to the family's rescue and offered to accompany NC's defiant daughter to Chambal for a meeting with the prospective groom.

The train journey was tense, Mummy told us. The scare of dacoits and the thought of meeting her future husband terrified and thrilled her at the same time. They arrived at the engineer's house, travel weary, on the third day, and started back for Warangal the very next afternoon. NC was waiting anxiously for his daughter's return.

"There is no way I am marrying that man," Mummy declared upon returning home, and there was no changing of minds. The wedding had to be called off, and NC sat in his easy chair with his head buried in his palms saying, "Nobody will marry you now. You have ruined your entire life."

Three months later, Mummy got engaged to another engineer, my father. He liked her spunk, he told her the first time he could speak to her alone.

A few months before my father died, I remember visiting a distant cousin's home with my parents and sister in Bombay. Our host came running out to meet us when he saw us drive up to tell us that the woman who's son Mummy had refused to marry all those years back was visiting too, and he did not want my parents to be embarrassed.

"So what," said Mummy. "Let her see the man I married."

When Daddy died, there were whispers about how evil that old woman was, suggesting that she had something to do with the tragedy in our lives. I have met a real life witch, I thought at that time, but educated and practical thinking squelched those silly whispers right away. Three days after Daddy's death, Mummy flew to Bangalore to visit his aging mother, my grandmother, who could not attend the funeral. It is funny that I do not remember Mummy leaving, but do remember going to the airport with my Uncles when she returned. Some memories are just there and have stayed all these years, whereas I cannot recall some events because they never turned into memories.

And then there are images that I want to forget, like that of my mother standing at the top of the stairs and sobbing, that refuses to go away. There are flashes in my mind when I see her engulfed in grief. The very first time we visited my younger aunt in Bangalore after my father's death is when I saw my mother suffer once again. She had imposed rules upon herself by refusing to wear a red *bindi*. Red was the color of fertility and marriage and she was a widow now. She wore only minimal jewelry, and resorted to simple saris.

In Bangalore, we visited my aunt's relatives on her husband's side of the family, and when it came time to leave, the hostess offered the *kumkum*—the red powder *bindi* that all married Hindu women apply to their foreheads—to all the women present and not to my mother as she was not entitled to it. This unleashed extreme fury, hurt, and a feeling of insult in my mother, and she gave into her grief by taking to her bed upon returning home and refusing to leave for the next two days. I can see my Uncle now, sitting by her and patting her head and trying to pacify her, but she would not relent.

"Never ever do this to anyone Suppy," she would tell me time and time again after that as Shammi and I were growing up. "It does not matter if the person visiting you has a husband or not, if you offer the *kumkum* to one, you offer it to everyone." I have of course taken the easy way out—I do not offer it to anyone. I am a devout Hindu, but this does not mean that I agree with all the customs and traditions, and because of what this particular South Indian custom did to my mother, I have an aversion to it.

When Mummy married and entered her husband's house, she went into a joint family that consisted of my father's older brother and his wife, his youngest sister who was not yet married, his mother, and his mother's old aunt who had been a child widow. As a very young girl, this old aunt had been married but not sent to her husband's house, as she had not attained puberty. And before that could happen, illness had killed her young husband, which left her a widow, at probably under the age of ten. She died soon after

I was born, and I rely on my mother's memories of her and her life, left to the mercy of relatives. What a difference a few decades make, I would think when I compared this aunt to my mother.

When I think of a traditional Hindu widow, I think of this great aunt of mine and of those numerous old widows who live in the holy city of Benares. Those women who have shaved their heads in grief and keep it covered with their saris. I think of the saris they wear in muted colors and made of simple cotton. In some communities, widows are not allowed to wear blouses with their saris. Why? Their saris are always wrapped around their bodies, and they are expected to spend the rest of their lives in prayer and meditation. And then I scold myself for even thinking that anyone in my family will be reduced to that. We are the educated class and we are beyond that, I tell myself. All that I have seen of those Benares widows is what is depicted in movies. I have not been there myself, and there is a distance that makes me feel superior. I look down upon families who abandon their old widows on the *ghats* of the holy Ganges.

Mummy had neither the time nor the tolerance for tradition. In its third decade after Independence, India was moving forward towards progressive thought in the '70s, and Mummy had to pick up where Daddy had left off and continue to raise her two girls. Daddy's death had accelerated our growing process, and she expected more from us physically and emotionally than she would have otherwise. She had wanted to be a workingwoman all her life, and now suddenly she had no choice but to become one. She was the breadwinner, the decision maker, the father, the mother, and the head of our tiny family.

What would have happened if she had demurely agreed to marry the Chambal Valley Engineer? I do not know and do not care. She would not have been my mother then, and I am sure she has not once regretted the ten short years she had with my father. Tara is the Hindi word for "star," and my father's death just made this star shine a bit brighter.

Amma...My Grandmother

Amma's migraine headaches were a big part of our lives as Shammi and I navigated our teenage years. Amma made our home her own after Daddy died. It was more of a home base for her, for she often left to visit her other children, my two uncles and one aunt in Hyderabad and Bangalore in South India. But she would always come back, and spend the major part of each year with us. Mummy always made sure that Amma went south during the winter months, as she was not used to Jaipur's cold weather.

Amma was a tiny person. She was of average height for an Indian woman, but painfully thin; at least from the time that I remember. This resulted in the skin on her hands hanging a little loose, and I remember as a child playing with the big bluish green vein that ran down her hand and ended just before the middle finger beyond her wrist. It would be nice to poke it here and there and watch it move and give way under my prodding finger. Amma did not mind. She would just smile and show me the vein in her other hand and let me play with that too. Her long thinning hair was almost all gray, and had been so for a long time, I was told, because of years of intense headaches. She parted her hair right in the middle and tied it in a little chignon at the nape of her neck. This had been her hairstyle since the time she got married; it was just that the chignon was the size of a grapefruit when she got married, and the size of a walnut by the time she died.

Not once in her eighty-two years did Amma wear a cotton or nylon sari. It was always a silk one, and when my grandfather was alive, it was heavy silk from the looms of Dharmavaram or Kanjeevaram with gold thread or *zari* in it. I see the black and white photograph of my grandparents that all her children and grandchildren have now, and try to picture it in color. NC was a big man, a little more than six feet tall and hefty. He stands in the picture with a half-sleeve shirt, a light colored woolen vest, and trousers. He wears glasses, and his forehead is lined vertically with the *Sricharanu* that both my grandfathers applied religiously. He stands with his palms linked casually in front of him and he towers over Amma standing to his left. Amma wears a big round *bindi* on her forehead that I know is red. Her sari pulloo is draped around her shoulders. She wears glasses too, and on the right side of her nose is a big diamond stud. It is the traditional South Indian one, a single stone flanked on the bottom with a semi-circle of three additional stones. Around her neck is a thick gold chain with a huge diamond pendant.

My grandfather was a medical doctor who pampered Amma, his second wife. He had lost the first one to complications during childbirth after she had given birth to two healthy boys, so NC was thirty two and Amma was sixteen when they married. She was closer in age and height to her stepsons than her husband. NC and Amma had five children together, two boys and three girls in quick succession. Mummy loves to tell the story that by the time Amma came back from her parents' house—all girls went to their parents' house to give birth—after each confinement, the older children would forget their father and had to get to know him all over again. And very soon it would be time to go back for the birth of another child. Mummy was the next to the last child, and she inherited her father's bold nature and other physical attributes.

Amma did not discipline her children, or rather she did not know how to. All that was left to NC. Her only attempt at trying to stop her kids from killing each other was, "I am going to tell your father all about this." Even though NC was strict, he was extremely indulgent and very progressive for the times, and he

56

particularly doted on his three daughters. Fluent in Tamil, Telugu, Hindi, Kannada, Marathi, and English, he was an intelligent and tolerant man. During the Hindu-Muslim riots in the mid-'50s, NC's Muslim patients trusted him enough to hand over all their gold jewelry and money to him for safe keeping.

Just as Amma's headaches dominate my childhood memories, so do Mummy's. When did these headaches start? No one knows. NC, being a doctor, treated Amma himself, and for the longest time had German medicines mailed to their house. Nothing helped. In Jaipur, long after my grandfather was gone, long after Daddy died, the headaches continued with a vengeance. In fact, Amma was never without a headache. It was part of her daily life. Time and time again, it just intensified. Amma loved to theorize upon what triggered them. In the summers, when the smell of ripe mangoes filled the air, she would give in to the urge and eat one or maybe two after lunch. Amma often blamed her headaches upon these mangoes.

"I get an upset stomach whenever I eat mangoes," she would say, "and an upset stomach is bad for my head."

Each onset of a migraine would be preceded by her suddenly becoming very quiet. She would wake up later than usual and not want anything to eat. "Just some strong coffee," she would tell Mummy. Very soon, Amma would have a strip of white cloth tied around her forehead, looking more like a Japanese Samurai than an Indian grandmother, and she would yank it tighter every so often. And then she would take to the bed. Mummy would draw all the curtains so there would be no light in the room. The door to her room would be shut, and from what I could see whenever Mummy went in, Amma would be on the bed face down. She would be in a fetal position, her knees bent and folded under her stomach and only her forehead resting on the pillow. And I could hear her moan.

For Shammi and me, it was scary to see Amma so helpless. Amma, who cooked for us and made all those nice goodies, was in intense pain now. She would consume no food during her attack—just coffee and more coffee, and upon Mummy's insistence, maybe some fruit juice. We tried to be very quiet, and that is all that we could do to help. After a couple of days like this, she would suddenly emerge from the room, her forehead still tied with the piece of cloth, her gray hair disheveled, her eyes sunken further into the hollows above her cheek bones, and say that it was better now. Amma would look thinner and smaller and ten years older at that moment. A hot bath and hot food would follow, and we were on the road to getting our old Amma back. Until the next attack, that is.

They say migraine headaches run in families. Every time I had a headache during my teenage years, I thought I had inherited Amma's migraine. None of her children suffer from the dreaded malady, however, nor do her many grandchildren. I read all about headaches now, as a grown woman, and try to remember what it must have been like for my grandmother. I know now why Mummy always made Amma's room dark. She definitely had photophobia, aversion to light, during the attacks. There was nausea too, as Amma would complain about her stomach churning. Having been married to a doctor for so long, Amma must have picked up that food allergies can trigger a migraine. She always found fault with whatever she had eaten just before the attack.

Amma was the quintessential grandmother for Shammi and me. She was with Mummy when she was pregnant with both of us, and helped look after us as newborns. I remember vividly the hot and humid summers of our childhood when our backs would be covered with prickly heat rashes. We would sit in front of Amma with our frocks bunched up to our necks so she could rub Nycil powder on it. Amma's hands were perfect for the job. They were not soft, and that very roughness was heavenly. As she gently massaged our backs with the powder, the calloused skin of her palms soothed the itching. When the skin between our toes itched, it was Amma we ran to so she could rub the area with her fingers.

When Mummy was growing up in Warangal, Amma did not have to cook. Their male cook, Ayyagaru, would arrive early in the morning and leave only after dinner had been prepared. Even though Amma had been married for thirty years, she was only in her mid-forties when my grandfather died, and it was then that she started cooking. Especially when she came to live with us in Jaipur. Mummy worked, and this was Amma's way of helping. When we left for school it was she who gave us breakfast, and when we returned home, we ate snacks prepared by her. Those were the days when Mummy hardly cooked. It was always Amma's cooking and it was good. "Ayyagaru made it this way," she would say remembering her old cook when she made tasty *Murku* or spicy *Tengavadai*, rice flour savories for our after school snack. Amma's *Gojju*, a sweet and spicy curry made from tomatoes, was out of this world. Her best was the one she made with okra. She would be generous with the red peppers, and with *Chappatis* and yogurt, it made for a heavenly meal. Sunday mornings, for a special treat, she would give me half a cup of coffee in which I would put *Tenkol*, another South Indian savory made from rice and lentil flour, and devour it with a spoon.

Amma operated on the premise that her grandchildren could do no wrong. She never applied that to her own children or even other children the same age as her grandchildren. All her life she had been dominated by strong willed people—her husband was the authority while her children were growing up, and now it was my mother who had the final say in our house. Amma was mild and soft-spoken, yet she could state her opinions with conviction and a certain degree of stubbornness. This came in handy when she spoke up for us. This trait lasted well into the adulthood of all her grandchildren, and was then transferred to benefit her great-grandchildren. In her early seventies when the great-grandchildren started arriving, she looked after them with more love than she gave each previous generation. It is with so much pride that I look back now and know that not only was she a grandmother to me, she was one to my children also.

Amma died six months after her eighty-second birthday. In the strictest sense we had lost her two years before, when one day she woke up and couldn't get out of bed. She was not the same mentally after that. In her confused state of mind, relationships changed—I became my mother and my mother became *her* mother. Amma's parents and all of her siblings, all of them long dead by now, came back to life, and she constantly talked about them and wanted only them.

"My mother is coming back from her pilgrimage today," she told me with great conviction once, when I was visiting home a year before we lost her. "Has my brother gone to the railway station to get her?"

When she looked at Anil, we knew that she had no idea that he was my husband, and she smiled politely at him, the type of smile she reserved for strangers. My children, whom she had so lovingly carried as babies, she ignored.

NC, whom she had remembered almost every day, was now truly gone. Although she had the paranoia that one of her daughters-in-law—one of my most loving aunts—was trying to beat her, and that someone was constantly trying to attack one of her grandchildren, she forgot the rest of us. She had become a child once more, and forgot that she was a grandmother.

It is truly amazing how many changes just a generation brings about. Mummy is a very different grandmother to my children than Amma was to Shammi and me. My mother is an independent, workingwoman, who cannot spend too much time at home or in the kitchen. On the other hand, Amma was always home, and most of that time was spent in the kitchen cooking for us.

Surprisingly, however, despite her complete loss of memory, Amma did not forget her wonderful recipes.

"Amma, can you please tell me how to make that almond chutney?" Mummy would ask, and Amma would rattle off the method without missing any of the ingredients. But, she forgot how to eat, she forgot how to drape a *sari*, she forgot how to bathe, and most importantly, she forgot that she had headaches. Amma was finally rid of her migraines.

Growing Up

On Sundays, Mummy, Shammi, and I—and Amma, if she was visiting us—truly had the whole house to ourselves. In the rooms that were used as classrooms, the furniture was stacked up against the corner, and the floor had been swept and mopped clean. Just for that day, the entire building was our house and not a school. However early I woke up on those days, I always found Amma in the kitchen cooking something. She loved to make snacks and sweets for us to munch on for the rest of the week. I always woke up to the aroma of freshly brewed coffee, and even though Shammi and I were not old enough to drink it, Mummy let us have a little bit only on those mornings. She called it a small dose, and always had Glucose-D cookies for us to dip in the coffee, which melted in our mouths. Dipping those cookies in the coffee was an art by itself, as they had to stay submerged in the hot brew just long enough. A fraction of a second more and they would break off and be at the bottom of the cup. On the other hand, if they were not dipped long enough, then they were too crunchy in our mouths and that was not nice. Shammi and I could finish the entire packet in one sitting. If there were no cookies, then Mummy had fresh bread to dip in the coffee. Of course, to dip the bread we needed more coffee we told Mummy, and her solution was to heat a cup of milk and add sugar and a little bit of the coffee from the steel percolator to it. Shammi and I drank hot milk with the flavor of freshly brewed coffee.

One Sunday, as usual, I was in a hurry to have my small dose, so I brushed my teeth and went to the toilet. The first thing I saw when I squatted on the Indian style W.C. was blood. It was October of 1972, I was eleven years and three months old, and Daddy had missed seeing his first-born grow up by a mere fifteen months.

My mother had prepared me for my first menstrual period. Sometime after my eleventh birthday, she had called me to the bedroom and explained everything, saying that in her family, periods come early and leave late. Amma, her own mother, she said, had failed to do so, and when her own period came, she did not tell anyone for the longest time thinking that she had a terrible disease and would die soon. She had vowed then, that if she had daughters, they would know about menstruation the proper way. She showed me what a sanitary pad looked like and let me feel it. Those days, the local market in Jaipur had only one brand—*Carefree*.

The summer before my first period, Shammi and I had visited my Vimmu Aunty in Delhi. Mummy had sent us there so we could spend a couple of weeks with our cousins. This was the aunt that all of us—Mummy, Daddy, Shammi, and I—had visited when she lived in the state of Assam, the year before Daddy died. We had taken the train to Calcutta, flown to Gauhati, and then traveled by car to Shillong where my uncle was stationed in the Air Force. That was the last vacation we took as a family, the end to the photographic record of Daddy's life.

I often browsed through the black and white photographs from that trip and to see his handsome face again, his upper lip framed by a thin moustache. I could not see his eyes for he wore dark sunglasses. Sitting on a huge boulder on a hilltop with Shammi and myself on either side, his arms encircled us, pulling us towards him. It was cold up there, but he wore only a shirt. I remember Mummy taking that photograph. For all of us he will always be as old as he was in those vacation photographs taken in Shillong. No sign of ill health, no clue that his heart would give way very soon, breaking ours in the process. That first summer in Jaipur, Mummy wanted us to visit the same aunt once again, another way of keeping Daddy's memory alive—by being close to his family.

The day before we left Delhi to head back home, I was with Vimmu Aunty in the kitchen, when Shammi came running to me wanting to know what I had in the small plastic bag that she was waving above her head.

"Give that to me," I snapped and took it back to the suitcase.

Vimmu Aunty followed me. "What is it Suppy?"

"Just sanitary pads," I said sheepishly.

"I didn't know you had your period," she was amazed. "Chandrika just had her first one a few months back."

"I don't have mine yet," I explained. "Mummy just thought that I should be ready, if I were to have it here."

I was very calm when I saw the blood and a bit excited too. I called Mummy into the toilet and told her. She said nothing, but returned with the sanitary pad and the thin elastic belt that held it in place. Our local market did not carry the self-adhesive variety. By the time I came out, Amma knew. Mummy made me sit down and brought my coffee to me. I could feel her excitement, but also saw the worry in her eyes.

"No running around for a few days Suppy," she said. "No school too as this is your first time."

I was thrilled.

Amma hovered around me, showing concern but not referring to the period. Mummy immediately called Jayu Aunty to tell her. Of course, she then promptly phoned her other sister, my Rama Aunty, in Bangalore too. On Sundays, the long distance calling rates were reduced.

"Are you having stomach cramps?" Mummy asked time and time again. Having never experienced menstrual cramps, I almost wished them upon myself so Mummy could fuss over me some more.

My father's death had forced me to grow up in a hurry

emotionally, and now my body was conforming to that. The very evening before I had my first period, my mother had gone to the market, and upon her return had called me to her and explained that as I was developing very fast physically, she thought it was high time that I wore a bra.

"Look Suppy, I have a nice lacy one for you," she had tried to excite me into wearing it.

It was a perfect fit, and I felt all grown up. It felt funny to have something tight around my chest, and I could not help running my hands around my body and feeling it under my T-shirt. I had felt self-conscious walking about the house after that, thinking that my still developing breasts were being held up too high by the bra.

Shammi was eight when all these changes were happening to my body, and blissfully unaware of it. Wearing my first bra and having my first period made me feel closer to my mother in age rather than to my younger sister. For Mummy, this was a bittersweet time—she was excited, but did not have Daddy to share her joy with.

Mummy loved to tell us that when Daddy returned from a year's stay in Germany when I was a baby, he brought back a black bra for her amongst other gifts. Some years later, I had walked into her room once, and finding the bra on the bed had held it up against my four-year-old chest, while admiring myself in the dressing table mirror. Daddy had laughed out aloud, telling Mummy that he could not wait to have "his girls" grow up.

"You can have that when you are a big girl, Suppy," Mummy had teased me then. She never wore that black bra. "It was padded," she told me in disgust when I started wearing one.

Jayu Aunty, a mother of two boys, was also very excited about my attaining puberty. She came over almost immediately that day. I was one of the oldest amongst the grandchildren in Amma's family, and this was a major event.

"What would you like for a gift, Suppy dear?" Jayu Aunty asked.

I was embarrassed.

"I do not need a gift for this," I protested.

"It is the custom," she said. "I would love to give you something."

"That's O.K. Jayu Aunty," I replied magnanimously, "you can give me something next month."

Mummy, Amma, and Jayu Aunty burst out laughing.

"You get something only the first time Suppy," Mummy explained. "Not every time you get a period."

When Mummy was growing up, it was the custom in South India to have a big celebration when a girl entered puberty, I was told. Only ladies are invited to this ceremony and the girl receives plenty of gifts.

"How silly," I protested vehemently. Why would one want to advertise the event?

"I am telling only my brothers and sisters, Suppy," Mummy assured me. "Not the whole world." Somehow I got the feeling that she would have loved to shout it from the rooftop.

One main restriction, Mummy told me, was that I could not go into any temple during this time every month. It was unholy to touch God, to enter the sanctum sanctorum. I was outraged.

"God does not mind," I had tried to argue. But it was the Hindu custom that we adhered to very strictly in our house, and Mummy would not budge. Customs and traditions become ingrained in us to such an extent that to this day I follow this restriction without questioning its logic.

Amma was a bit lax when it came to rules, but when my other grandmother— Daddy's mother—visited us in Jaipur, I could not even enter the kitchen during my period. I was too young to ask why, and looked on the bright side. I could now, for a few days at least, have Shammi do things for me. So, just for those three or four days, I felt thirsty very often, and of course had sudden pangs of hunger, much to my sister's annoyance.

"Suppy is handling it very well," Mummy told Jayu Aunty proudly that day in October. "She is not complaining at all."

Three days after this big event, three days after having to sit at home and not being allowed to go anywhere, was a family friend's wedding to which all of us had been invited. The only hitch now was that I was right smack in the middle of my first period, and Mummy decided that we could not go. I had looked forward to this wedding for a while now, and pleaded with her, telling her I would be careful until she finally relented. I wore nylon slacks, and a short *kurta* for a top that had a gold thread embroidered border at the end of the sleeves and around the neck. I wore leather *jooties* on my feet that were embroidered with gold thread too. These slip-on shoes were characteristically flat and very comfortable. At the wedding, I was careful when I sat, and did not walk fast. Jayu Aunty and Mummy hovered over me, concerned. It was silly, but I enjoyed it.

All my uncles and aunts sent me money. My mother used it up to buy a nice pair of gold and pearl earrings, and I wore them for the first time, nine years later, on my wedding day.

All the fuss that accompanied my first period soon died down. The second one did not happen until a few months later, and by then all of us were thoroughly used to the fact that I had started menstruating. The practical problems that accompany a period, however, started with my second one.

Every month, during my period, I was most uncomfortable in my school uniform—the royal blue box-pleated skirt. It felt too short, and I kept tugging at it, trying to make it longer. Climbing into the *tonga*—the horse-driven buggy—that took us to school, I had to be careful and hold my skirt close to me. The ride in the *tonga* was bumpy, and I had to sit on the edge of the seat, afraid that I would stain my skirt.

At school, we had long benches, with backs and arms, and desks in each classroom. When I sat, I always adjusted my skirt so as not to sit on it. It was an all-girls school, and I had seen the others doing this. When I was in doubt, I would ask one of my friends to look down my back to see if everything was O.K.

In the 6th grade, my mother deemed that I was old enough to ride my bike to school with my friends. Shammi still rode the tonga, but I felt very important getting my shiny green, brand new ladies bicycle out and strapping my school bag to the back of it. Off I went to a friend's house on the way, where I would stand outside her gate and ring the bell on the bicycle. Together then, we would go to a third friend's house and very soon we had our own bicycle group.

It was a good fifteen-minute ride to school, and I loved it. During my period, I couldn't sit on the bike as I did on the school bench—the skirt would fly up. So I had to be careful not to move too much on the seat, and when I got off, I instinctively looked back and down to see if all was fine. On the way home I did not care. Even if something were amiss, I could change right away.

In those beginning years, I did not get my period regularly, and this worried Mummy. In fact, it scared her. One day she called me to her and said in a very serious tone:

"Suppy dear, you know that you should not let anyone touch you?"

I was perplexed and embarrassed. "Of course, Mummy," I said, trying to ward off any further discussion on this matter.

"I am serious, Suppy," she continued. "You will tell me if something like that happens, won't you?" she persisted.

"Yes, Mummy," I said. "Don't be silly."

I could see her relief a few days later when I told her that I had my period.

In my own house now, I do not light he *diyas* for *those* four or five days at my little altar as I do every other day of the month, and I do not go to the temple. Anil used to get annoyed about this silly custom, but he is resigned to it now and does not question it. By the time our older son realized that I was not lighting the daily lamps, he had had enough Human Growth and Development classes at school. When he asked why, I simply told him that I was having my period and explained our custom without having to tell him what a menstrual period was.

As the mother of three boys now, I do not have to deal with the same things that my mother had to. Shammi, on the other hand, is the mother of two little girls, and I hope she has learnt a few valuable lessons about dealing with a daughter's period from our mother.

The excitement about my first period, all those years back, was a wave that lifted us out, for a short time, from our everyday life; a life that we—Mummy, Shammi, and I—were trying to create without Daddy. And Mummy, as a single parent, had to do it all alone. When she was troubled, she was all alone, and when she was excited, she was all alone.

Mummy still worries about us.

"Just because you have children of your own does not mean that I stop worrying about *my* children," she says.

There was a time, a few years after my marriage, when she worried that I was not getting pregnant. Now, life has turned full circle, and just as she did when I was a teenager, she is back to worrying that I *shall* become pregnant.

"It is too late now, Suppy," she says, "you have three wonderful boys. No more."

Evenings on Sunder Marg

When the hot summer days gave way to cool evenings, it was as if a collective sigh of relief went around all the houses on *Sunder Marg* in those early years, soon after we became a newly minted independent family of three. Days were perpetually long, and the hustle and bustle of the evenings were in sharp contrast to the laziness of the super heated afternoons. The children on our *marg* or street would have been home from school for a while and taken their afternoon nap or finished their homework or whatever else they did after coming home from school. The intense desert heat of Jaipur put everyone in a stupor in the afternoons. So while the breadwinners were at work yawning and fidgeting with their collars, their households took part in the afternoon siesta. Servants slept and housewives slept; grandparents slept, and even dogs and cats slept. If God Almighty had decided to pay a visit to *Sunder Marg* on any summer afternoon, even He would have been tempted to take a nap after finding the street deserted with not a soul stirring.

In our house, my father's untimely death had made my mother the breadwinner, and when Blue Bells closed down each afternoon, it was a time for cleaning. *Jamadaars* with massive brooms swept the concrete compound outside the building, while the other servants swept and mopped the floor inside. Mummy never had time for a leisurely nap. As our living quarters were in the school building itself, she would steal a few quick winks in the easy chair in her bedroom before waking up all refreshed to start her afternoon chores.

This easy chair was an armchair with a wooden frame

that supported a canvas or nylon hammock. When you sat in it, the hammock cradled you, and you were half-reclining. Mummy inherited two of these chairs from her father's house in Warangal, and she thought they were the most comfortable pieces of furniture in the whole world. Amma, when she was visiting us, often dozed off in the other one. Apart from being very comfortable, Mummy's premise was that taking a short nap in the easy chair did not crush her crisply starched cotton sari, which actually lying on a bed would destroy. The only upkeep for these huge chairs was an occasional replacement of the hammock, which would wear out with the weight.

The servants would often interrupt these mini-naps, short as they were, asking for an advance in their pay or asking for a leave of absence. Shammi and I, as children, knew better than to disturb Mummy from these power naps, and did our best to keep them uninterrupted. After a hard day's work, this respite was important to Mummy, and I had seen her shouting at the servants if disturbed, something that I wanted to avoid at all cost.

In the summer, in Jaipur, huge monstrosities called desert coolers could be seen sticking out from most windows in each house. These coolers made the afternoon siestas, short or long, more comfortable. Not credited with complexity in design, desert coolers were simple, square boxes made of aluminum, and placed on an iron stand. The side of the square that fitted in the window had a grill through which we could see the four-blade fan facing the room. The other three sides of the cooler had a grill too, but were padded on the inside with a fragrant straw-like substance called *khus*. The bottom of the box had to be filled with water, and when turned on, small narrow pipes carried this water to the three sides and dripped it slowly on the *khus* while the fan sucked in hot air from the outside and pushed the water-cooled fragrant air into the room. These coolers were not effective in humid temperatures, but for Jaipur's dry desert heat months from April until June, they were a boon, and the fresh air they blew into the rooms was better than air-conditioning. Afternoon naps with these desert coolers on were made easier because the loud noise they made blocked any coming from the street outside and sounded like a giant's lullaby.

As the hot afternoons gave way to the cooler evenings, the arrival of the maid to clean the dishes from lunch stirred up the household. Also, it was time to have a hot cup of late-afternoon-early-evening tea, which was a tradition year-round. Tea woke people up and prepared them for the evening's activities. Mummy was actually a coffee lover, but the afternoon cup of tea has been a ritual that has been faithfully followed throughout the years. One of the first things Shammi and I learnt as we grew up was to make tea, and Mummy readily relinquished this chore to us.

The art of tea making is one legacy that did not remain with the common man when we Indians drove the British out in 1947. In India, in most households, tea is not brewed in the dainty English way by using teapots. Instead, water is boiled first in a saucepan on the stove to which we add a good measure of strong tea, usually a blend of leaves that is grown in Darjeeling and sold by Lipton. The hot water immediately turns a rich chocolate brown, and to this is added milk and sugar. In a final act, this strong brew is poured into cups through a strainer to keep the tealeaves out. This strong, sweet, and thick caffeine rich *chai* can be quite addictive. Mummy loved to tell us about the family tailor in her parents' house. He was asked periodically throughout the year to come home and sew clothes and do other repairs as required. The first thing he asked my grandmother when he settled down to his work was, "Have you had tea?" Amma of course immediately understood this broad hint, and had the family cook make the tailor a large steaming cup of hot and sweet tea. To this day, whenever Shammi and I feel like having tea, we ask Mummy with a straight face, "Have you had tea?"

Being from the south, where coffee drinking is more popular, Mummy was more particular while buying coffee. She did not mind going all the way to Patwari Brothers on Mirza Ismail Road, the only store that sold coffee, freshly ground to order, in Jaipur then. The right amount of chicory had to be added while grinding the roasted beans to get to the perfect strength. The strong heady aroma of fresh coffee in our house reinforced the fact that we were South Indians living in Northern tea-drinking India. For Mummy, a dose of coffee, as she called it, was always welcome and she could, if need be, do away with tea altogether.

Desert sand heats fast and cools equally fast. Even though Jaipur was a metropolis where streets had been paved, the city retained the inherent quality of the earth it lay upon. As the sun set, it took the heat with it. The noisy desert coolers that we had on inside the house were turned off, and it was nice to come out and sit in the verandah with a book, or the daily newspaper.

My love for many authors started in those early teenage years. Up until then it had only been Enid Blyton with her series—*The Secret Seven, The Five Findouters, The Famous Five,* and others. While reading Enid Blyton, I had fantasized about being part of an English family eating scones and sandwiches for tea. What were scones anyway? They sounded delicious! The everyday Indian food that we ate—*roti, dal,* rice, curry—lacked the glamour and sophistication that eating a hot scone with melted butter on it had. And then there were all those girls in Enid Blyton books who wore smart uniforms and went to boarding school in the *Mallory Towers* series. How I wished to be there with them! Or at least have friends like Larry, Pip, Betty, Fatty, and Daisy and solve mysteries like them. I imagined myself on some lonely island of the British Isles caught by smugglers and trying to escape along with my imaginary dog.

From where I sat on the verandah of our house, I could see Moti Doongri in the not so distant horizon. It was a small hillock with a huge fortress built on top belonging to Jaipur's royal family. Unlike other palaces that had been converted to luxury hotels, to support the lavish lifestyles of the royals or taken over by the government after Independence, this fort remained private property, and always had an aura of mystery about it. No one could tell us how it was inside, and I made this my imaginary case to solve. Just as the children in Enid Blyton's mysteries saw flashing lights from abandoned lighthouses, I saw someone signaling from the top of Moti Doongri. My band of sleuths consisted of Shammi and me of course, and also Sanju and Jaideep, our cousins. And we had to have Kalu, the dog, instead of Buster. On the base of Moti Doongri is a Ganesh temple that we went to religiously every week, and I would look up at the old fort above or through the locked gates to the driveway that wound up the hill and just wonder.

When I outgrew Enid Blyton and got over my desire for eating a scone and going to a boarding school and solving a mystery, I read Jane Austen, Emily Brontë, and her sister Charlotte. I devoured *Wuthering Heights* and enjoyed Alexander Dumas's *The Three Musketeers*. Each and every one of Agatha Christie's mysteries fascinated me, as did Sherlock Holmes and his Mr. Watson. I get a funny eerie feeling even now when I think of *The Hound of the Baskervilles*, and when I see the movie *Little Women* I say to myself, "I *know* these people. I grew up with them. I *want* to be Jo." I loved the way the D'Urberville in Tess's last name sounded, and I said it over and over again with rounded lips and a rolling tongue, and I practiced saying Thomas by leaving out the 'h' in his first name in the proper British way while wondering what the word "madding" meant. The unforgettable lines of Daphne du Maurier's *Rebecca,* when the strange glow over the horizon turns out to be Manderley burning, still ring in my ears. To this day, when I return after an extended trip, I scan the skies as I come closer to home. Will I see an orange glow?

And then I entered the realm of evening gowns and debutante balls with Barbara Cartland's romances. Her heroes were tall, dark, and handsome and they were so cruel and so passionate. I was lost in a world far away in time and distance, but could never imagine myself in their place. I did not have the heart shaped face and high cheekbones and rosy lips of those heroines, and was of the wrong color anyway. I also found myself addicted to Mills & Boon romances. I could finish one of those books in two days flat, and I read and reread the last few pages where the girl finally succumbs to the charms of her wild lover.

As long as it did not interfere with schoolwork, Mummy did nothing to discourage my passion for reading. She did, however, make sure Shammi and I learnt the basics of cooking a simple meal. Lunch was usually the bigger meal of the day, and we did not give much thought to dinner, so preparing it was left for later. Dinner in our house was usually leftovers with one fresh item added. And we ate late—nobody thought about eating before nine at the very earliest. Mummy was a good cook, but in those beginning years of the '70s, after Daddy's death, weekday cooking was usually not given much importance, and Shammi and I did not care as Mummy had schoolwork in the evenings to complete. She would sit in the verandah with us with her accounts folder or check homework assignments from the English classes she taught.

For the first few summers after we moved to the house on *Sunder Marg*, Mummy, Shammi, Amma, and I would sleep on the terrace above at night, as we did not have a lawn outside our house like the others in our neighborhood. Each house had a compound wall with a gate that was locked at night. For us, the cool night air was a change from the oppression of the heat inside, and the rising sun did not bother us as we had to be up at the crack of dawn anyway to start the new day. For sleeping on the terrace we had cots called *charpahis*, which literally means four legs. The four legs of the cot were held together by canvas strips that were woven together to form a base on which we would spread a thin mattress and then put a sheet on it. Lying on these cots and looking up at the sky above with its millions of twinkling stars on mid-summer nights was an exhilarating experience, and if the mosquitoes bothered us then we had huge nets that went over these cots supported by a frame of their own. When we were ready for bed, we crawled under these nets very carefully so as not to let a single mosquito in and then tucked the ends of the net under the mattress. In the daytime we would fold the sheets, roll the mattresses, and pile up these *charpahis* against the wall of the landing on the second floor that led out to the terrace.

Often I would come up later than the others if I had to study for a test or finish homework. Once Mummy came down to our bedroom and found me with an open science book on my lap that was actually a cover for the smaller Barbara Cartland romance that I had been dying to finish. I had been caught and could do nothing but stare at her in horror. She gave me a hard cold look and said, "I am very disappointed, Suppy," before leaving the room. That night it took me a long time to go up to bed. This of course did not deter me from reading more of these passion filled romances. I just made sure that I did not give in to the temptation while doing homework.

This practice of sleeping on the terrace on clear summer nights in Jaipur did not last very many years for fear of safety. There were stories of houses being burglarized while everyone either slept on the terrace or on the lawn outside, and Mummy soon decided that we would sleep inside, heat or no heat.

Late afternoons and early evenings was also the time for vegetable vendors to do their rounds on *Sunder Marg* with their cartloads of fresh vegetables that they pushed by hand. These carts were on four wheels, and the vegetables had been bought from the wholesale market in the city and then sold to people like us who had no time to go to the market. Mummy made regular trips to the local market to buy vegetables, but would often get something from these mobile carts as well. These *thelas* often became the gathering place for the neighboring housewives as each one came out to haggle with the vendor over the price of the vegetables.

As we sat on the verandah in the evenings drinking tea or just reading something, it was fun to see who walked by on the street outside. Often it would be couples from the neighboring houses out on their evening stroll, and I imagined seeing Mummy and Daddy in their place. I would see the Banerjee family—father, mother, and two sons—leave in their white Fiat, and I would remember when Daddy, Mummy, Shammi, and I would drive to the market in our black Ambassador in Bombay. The marketplace was so busy that Daddy would park the car just outside the store so just Mummy could go in to buy provisions for the week. As a treat, Shammi and I would get sugar cigarettes with red tips that we would suck on and pretend to smoke in the back seat while Daddy actually smoked a real one in the front. When he inhaled, we inhaled, and when he exhaled, we did so too, making sure we held the cigarette just right and cocked our heads at the same angle to let the smoke out. At other times, we would get a packet of mint each, and we would have a competition as to who could hold on to these the longest.

But now we were a fragmented family, our lives very different from the big city life that we had left behind in Bombay. Jaipur was a smaller and quieter city.

"Mummy, here come Othello and Desdemona," I would whisper, much to my mother's horror, on the verandah of our house on *Sunder Marg* as I flaunted my knowledge of Shakespeare. Mr. and Mrs. Bhandari lived three houses down from ours, and each evening they would come out for a stroll around the neighborhood. He was big and dark complexioned with features that did nothing to flatter his appearance. She was petite and light-skinned, and with a big round red *bindi* on her forehead, she looked very pleasant. What a mismatched couple, I always thought, and the nicknames we gave them in our early teenage years stayed for good. Shammi and I, and eventually even Mummy never referred to them by their actual names.

And then of course we always had Mrs. Verma in the house opposite peering at us curiously through a gap in the big mango tree in her yard. A young widow living all alone, running a school, and raising two girls must have been the topic of many a discussion in the households all around us. Mrs. Verma kept track of who entered our house and who left with an unfriendly stare that we soon got used to. Mummy had neither the inclination nor the time to socialize with any of these nosy neighbors, and soon they got used to us and even looked up to Mummy in awe. The less educated and sophisticated ones around us referred to her as *Masterni*, a made-up female version of the English Master, while the more educated and cultured people around us called her Mrs. Satyan or *Taraji*, adding the honorific to her first name out of respect.

It is amazing how life forms a pattern for us and we fit right into it either out of necessity or simply because we like it that way. Mummy, Shammi, and I had left Daddy and the big city life behind in Bombay, and Jaipur was now truly our home. Even 1971's war with Pakistan with its tensions and upheavals had become a thing of the past, and people had become complacent once again. They soon forgot the thrill mixed with fright of air raid sirens, the impracticality of blackouts when everything had to be done by candlelight, and only war news whenever the radio was turned on. Television had just come to Jaipur in the early '70s, but the government-run stations had boring programs. We watched TV just for the daily news and the weekly movie on Sundays. Day in and day out, sitting out in the verandah in the evenings and watching life go by at an unhurried pace on *Sunder Marg* was more entertaining than any soap opera on TV. These mundane things that we took for granted then have become nostalgia for me now in my adult life. Sometimes, I want desperately to be back in those days, with the house just the way it was then, and Shammi and I young girls again and living with Mummy—just the three of us together in our house on *Sunder Marg*.

I try to recreate my childhood for my boys now. When they first started reading "chapter books," I promptly brought Enid Blytons from India for them to read, expecting to see the same excitement on their faces as they read the various mysteries. Their complete lack of interest deeply disappointed me. They could not identify with the English lifestyle described in the books. They did not know the foods, the language, the terminology, or the place. I was trying to thrust something foreign to my thoroughly American kids. Just out of curiosity, I tried to read what they liked, and had the same reaction that they had to my beloved Enid Blytons. But then, I am becoming American too. The drip coffee that I drink now in America is different from the percolator-brewed coffee of my childhood. The coffee that I buy here is more coarsely ground than what is required for the percolator, which spews out a strong brew. I am so used to what I have here that I do not much enjoy the coffee back home, and Mummy fails to understand why I cannot enjoy her strong coffee anymore.

It is the same with afternoon naps. I have always been averse to them, and never take them. Anil loves them, Shammi loves them, and Mummy still takes them. If ever I succumb to one, I wake up feeling depressed, as if there is a big weight on my head. In so many years of marriage, Anil has failed to understand this feeling, and continues to strongly advocate these naps on weekends.

Sundays on Sunder Marg

Throughout my teenage years, even though India and many parts of the outside world were going through various stages of political upheaval, life on *Sunder Marg* dragged on at an unhurried pace. Sundays on *Sunder Marg* were especially quiet. No early morning activity, no traffic, not even the ring from a lone bicycle. The street sweepers, too, took it easy and came a little late. They held their massive brooms made out of thin long sticks with both hands, and with the elegant grace of a dancer they moved their bodies from side to side as they swept the sand and gravel off the street. The swooshing sound their brooms made along with their monotonous chatter as they worked, often was the first activity on Sunday mornings. Ram Dhan was the head sweeper for our area. His group of workers was made up from his family. During the week, they worked as *Jamadaars* at the Government Hospital in the city. After cleaning the toilets and dirty floors of the hospital all week, this was a means to make some extra money. Each house on the street paid them monthly wages, and no other sweeper was allowed in "their" area. Ram Dhan's wife worked with him as he swept the street in front of our house. His son and daughter-in-law took care of the street to our left, while his two daughters swept the other side. Except for his wife, the other women used smaller brooms.

Many varieties of birds made their home in the trees that lined *Sunder Marg*, and somehow, even they knew that it was Sunday. There were harsh looking crows with their black and gray bodies, cawing incessantly. Then there were dull-colored sparrows constantly flitting from here to there like restless children who can never sit still. Shammi and I, however, were most interested in the mynahs with their bright yellow beaks. We used to instinctively kiss the tips of our fingers as many times as the number of mynahs spotted, saying under our breath, "one for sorrow" or "two for joy." This ended at seven birds, three being for a letter, four for a toy, five for silver, six for gold, and seven for a secret not to be told. As teenagers, it was too embarrassing to say it aloud, so we muttered it under our breaths. When more than seven mynahs swooped down into our yard, the finger kissing became redundant.

The birds on *Sunder Marg* would have a lazy morning too, waking up only when the *Jamadaars* arrived. The noise the brooms made and the dust that was dispelled with each stroke woke them up. In unison they would chirp and fly about in partnership with the dust, which could be seen in the rays of the morning sun. After the sweepers, the next visitor to our street would be the milkman with huge milk cans hanging on each side of his bicycle. He would stand outside each gate and ring his bell—a cue for a servant or housewife to run out with a vessel to get milk. The milkman's coming was the official start of the day, as morning tea could be made only after the milk had been boiled.

Soon to follow was the bread man. His arrival was very welcome to Shammi and me—he brought eggs, too, and also crème rolls, which were pastry puffs, conical in shape, filled with soft white fluffy cream that melted in our mouths. They were sinfully delicious and terribly unhealthy, but we did not care. Not everyone on the street ate eggs and bread for breakfast—a western concept. Mummy had always made omelets and toast for Sunday breakfast; even when we lived in Bombay, when Daddy was still with us. On other days we had cornflakes with sweetened warm milk, the only western cereal available in India then.

By the time the sweepers actually left *Sunder Marg*, the neighborhood was wide-awake. It would then be time for the maidservants to come to our house to clean—they never had Sundays off. There was one who came to sweep and mop the floor and one to clean dirty dishes from Saturday night's dinner and the Sunday morning breakfast. The only concession was that they came in a bit later than the other days. As they worked, they regaled us with gossip from the other houses they worked in, especially about houses where we neither knew the family nor did we care.

"*Baiji*," they would respectfully address Mummy, "Sharma *Behenji* is very stingy. I asked for an old sari and she refused to give it," one would say while sweeping the floor.

"They cook a lot of meat and fish in their house. I have told them that I cannot clean their utensils anymore," the other would say about another family that lived in *Tilak Nagar* but not on *Sunder Marg*.

One big reason for *Sunder Marg* being so quiet on Sundays was that Blue Bells was closed. No morning traffic of auto rickshaws, cycle rickshaws, scooters, and cars dropping kids off; no ringing of the school bell at the start and end of each day and at regular intervals in between heralding a change in class period; and no cacophony of kids jumping, running, and chatting during lunch break. The room that we used the most as a "family room," was a large enclosed verandah at the back of the house, which on school days was the Kindergarten classroom. The back wall of our weekend family room was a cement trellis through which sunlight streamed in. On hot summer evenings, this wall was a boon as we felt the cool night air; on cold winter nights it was a curse.

Apart from her imposing Principal's Desk and chair and a few chairs to receive parents, the big room at the front of the house had our nice *Divan* and two armchairs with end tables on each side, furniture that came with us when we moved here from Bombay. The *Divan's* colorful spread was a reminder of our holiday trip to visit Daddy's sister in Assam. The cushion covers had bouquets of flowers embroidered on them, showing off Mummy's talent during her "housewife" days when Shammi and I were babies. This living room opened out into the Kindergarten classroom at the back of the house, which in turn was flanked by our kitchen and bedroom on either side.

The one person the entire neighborhood was sure to hear on Sundays, was Mrs. Rastogi who lived next to us on our right, and the good Lord had provided her with a loud voice that was directly proportionate to her size. Mrs. Rastogi was unusually tall for an Indian woman. She was stout too, but not obese. She wore her sari the traditional *Rajasthani* way—the *pulloo* of her sari coming from behind and over the right shoulder and going back under her left arm. In keeping with tradition, she was quick to cover her head with the sari *pulloo* when men from her husband's family visited. She never ever forgot to cover her head, but often the *pulloo* would be bunched up around her neck and she would forget to cover her chest. The sari blouse that covered her sagging middle-aged breasts often had a few hooks missing, making even the women of the neighborhood want to look away in shame.

Mrs. Rastogi often started off Sundays by shouting at her husband and three good-for-nothing sons. She never ever shouted at her only daughter, but then she never ever talked to her either. That mother-daughter interaction, or rather the lack of it, was the first crude lesson in the psychology of relationships for me, especially since it was in sharp contrast to what Shammi and I had with our mother. Of course, Mummy could have her temper tantrums too. She could yell at us and use her single status to emotionally remind us of how difficult we were being, but thankfully such instances were rare and we always got over them. The other fights about clothes and studies and homework and grades were not a serious matter.

Our loud neighbor's oldest son would once in a while shout back at his mother, but none of us heard Mr. Rastogi or the other two sons or the daughter. Whenever these shouting matches occurred,

84

we could be sure that Mrs. Verma, who lived right opposite us—the matriarch of an equally dysfunctional family—would be standing at her compound wall, in the shade of the huge mango tree, straining to hear what was being said in the Rastogi household. Mrs. Rastogi and Mrs. Verma were not particularly fond of each other. Mrs. Verma had lost one young daughter to an illness, and this tragedy was followed by the suicide of another grown daughter, who burnt herself to death. This took a heavy toll on Mrs. Verma's state of mind. It had mentally affected her only son too, but three surviving girls were surprisingly normal. Both Mr. Verma and Mr. Rastogi found their wives to be intellectually incompatible. Mr. Verma worked as a librarian at the University and Mr. Rastogi was an official in the State Judiciary, and it was unlikely that their wives were even high school graduates. For all that she lacked in decorum, grace, and a cultured upbringing, Mrs. Rastogi had a sincere and kind heart. Mummy always had only nice things to say about her and expected us girls to afford her the proper respect. As for Mrs. Verma, we ignored her, as she was our crazy staring-at-us-from-behind-the mango-tree neighbor.

The State Bank of India leased the house to our left for the manager of its Jaipur branch. Every one and a half to two years, this manager would be transferred out, and a new one would arrive, making it difficult for us to have a lasting relationship with any of them. Anyway, because the family was provided with a chauffeur-driven Ambassador sedan and a security guard at the gate, they always thought of themselves as a step above all of their neighbors on the social ladder. They did not bother to become friends with the neighbors and in return, the neighbors left them alone. Mummy always had a nodding relationship with Mr. Manager, as all the successive ones respected her for single-handedly running the school and raising two daughters.

The radio was always on at our house on Sundays. It was nice to hear religious songs in the mornings on *Vividh Bharati*, the only nationally run radio station. The religious songs and hymns seemed right for that time of the morning instead of the film songs that we heard during the rest of the day. So we woke up to the polite yet monotonous voice of the announcer saying in Hindi,

"This is *Akaashvani's Vivid Bharati* on 202.5 kilohertz."

Mummy was always very regular about reading the newspaper. We got the English *Indian Express* for national news and the Hindi *Rajasthan Patrika* for local news. I read the English one only. In the Hindi one, I had a morbid interest in reading about who had died and whose third-day mourning ceremony was being announced. Only family and close friends went for the actual funeral and everyone else went on the third day, the official day to mourn. Other than the obituaries, it was tedious to read in Hindi as it was my second language at school.

Mummy was particular about many things, and one of them was ironing. Even though the *Dhobi* took all the sheets and saris and our *salwar kameez* and *churidars* and jeans, Mummy refused to give him her many blouses. She had me iron those along with any leftovers of mine, and this activity became a dreaded Sunday afternoon chore.

"I make you iron my blouses, not because I do not want to do it myself, but to teach you girls how to iron clothes properly," she would say when we complained. The same explanation applied for taking turns cleaning the refrigerator.

"You girls will thank me when you grow up and have households of your own to manage," she would say. Shammi and I, however, failed to see the logic behind these statements, and never tired of complaining.

The only relief while ironing was the Sunday afternoon movie on the radio. We had no TV at first, in those beginning years after moving to *Sunder Marg*, to watch movies at home. We heard them on the radio, instead, and as these were usually old movies that we had already seen in the theatres, it was easy to picture the action in our minds. So we could "see" the pain in the heartthrob Rajesh Khanna's face as he sang his sad song from *Kati Patang*, and "feel" his passion when he told a reluctant wide-hipped Asha Parekh how much he loved her. The movie on the radio was always interrupted periodically for ads. The same products again and again, the same jingles over and over. We no longer paid attention; we just hummed along. And then there was the ever-important news. Mummy always listened to the news. She had to find out what Indira Gandhi had to say that day, what Pakistan was up to now, and the latest on Nixon's Watergate scandal. News time was break time for me from ironing Mummy's many blouses.

Nothing much happened on those lazy Sundays during the years Shammi and I were growing up, yet so much happened. We actually did grow up. We learned to manage without Daddy. Mummy had taken over and she was doing just fine. Her school was popular and flourishing. She was earning enough to provide for us. We did not want for anything. We were by no means a "whole" family, yet we had survived.

I see yellow beaked birds outside my house in Fairfax sometimes, and instinctively count how many there are, knowing fully well that they have nothing to do with any luck or joy or sorrow or silver or gold or a letter. In fact, in this day of the Internet, I have stopped getting letters from my family! But just seeing those birds changes Heatherford Place into *Sunder Marg* for me for an instant. Of course I do not tell my boys about this finger kissing activity. When Shammi and I were children, this game was girl play, but now I am sure even the girls will shun it.

More than the birds, I miss not having a servant coming in every day to clean my dishes or someone coming to dust and sweep and mop everyday. What is luxury here is the way of life in India where the abundance of population makes human labor very cheap. When I first came to America, I would call home and say that

I missed the *Dhobi* who ironed our clothes more than my family. Every Sunday morning, the washerwoman would come to wash all our dirty clothes and linen and hang them on clotheslines to dry. Every Sunday evening, the *Dhobi* would come to take all the clothes that needed ironing. Mummy kept a separate *Dhobi* book where she would keep count of all the clothes he took and it was my job sometimes, to check off these items when he brought the clothes back in a couple of days.

Washing machines have replaced washerwomen now in India, and I like the convenience of not waiting for someone to have clean clothes, but also wonder about how many poor people have lost their means to earn a living because of an influx of these machines. The *Dhobi*, however, remains. I give him my cotton clothes to iron and also the boys' shorts and Anil's shirts, but I iron t-shirts and delicates myself, afraid that he will scorch these clothes with his heavy coal-burning iron.

The boys, oblivious to what gives me joy, take pleasure in shopping for cereal at the local market in Jaipur. The cornflakes of the '70s were a bit thinner than the flakes we get here in America now. My children eat Frosted Flakes—it is hard to describe to them the special place I have for cornflakes in sweetened warm milk. Now in Jaipur, the market is flooded with all varieties of Kellogg's and General Mills cereals and the boys find it hard to believe that I grew up without them.

Maharani Gayatri Devi Girls' Public School (MGD)

Sometime in the early part of 1973, Aparna, who came from a good upper middle-class family and who was a senior and a boarder at MGD, managed to sneak out of school periodically and meet with a young man she thought she had fallen in love with. Soon, she found herself pregnant. In a state of panic, her boyfriend sneaked her out of school and took her to a local quack for a quick abortion, where something went terribly wrong during the procedure and massive infection and poisoning spread through Aparna's sixteen-year-old body, killing her in the process. In the summer of 1973, this was big news in Jaipur, and the local *Rajasthan Patrika* covered it for days. Mrs. Rastogi, our neighbor, whispered loudly when she talked about this with my mother across the compound wall that separated our houses.

"I knew it!" she declared with conviction. "All the girls who go to that school are like that. Rich families—no character. Just imagine—getting pregnant and then trying to drop the baby! And then of course, dying. Shameful, shameful."

Mummy nodded and said nothing as she usually had no reaction to most of what Mrs. Rastogi said. She listened and then promptly ignored everything. Shammi and I learnt to do that too as we grew up. We smiled politely of course as Mrs. Rastogi went on and on. That very summer Mummy had decided that Shammi and I should shift schools from St. Angela Sophia to the more prestigious MGD—I would go into the seventh grade and Shammi would be in the fourth. Aparna's death did not make it easy for my mother as all her family and friends advised against sending her girls to a school where a scandal had so recently happened. But she was confident that she would raise her girls right and what had happened to one girl did not necessarily reflect on the character of the school as a whole.

I did not know Aparna, and apart from having a vague feeling of horror for the situation, I did not care. It was an exciting prospect—this changing of schools—and if Mummy thought that we needed to go there, it was fine with me. Locally, MGDians were a breed apart from the girls who attended the other schools, and soon Shammi and I were going to be a part of that group.

MGD was named for the Maharani of the Jaipur royal family. The beautiful Gayatri Devi was the daughter of the Maharajah of Cooch Behar in eastern India, and at the age of nineteen she met the young Man Singh—whose royal title was, Maharajah Sir Sawai Man Singh (II) Bahadur of Jaipur—while traveling in England, and fell in love. Her parents opposed the match as she would be Man Singh's third wife, but she would not listen. In pre-independence India, it was common for the royals to have several wives, and she knew that the first two were marriages of convenience. She knew she was his true first love, and she was right. When Gayatri Devi first came to her husband's home as a young bride in 1939, she could neither speak the native Marwari or Hindi, but she adjusted well and became a favorite of her subjects.

Man Singh was the last Maharajah of Jaipur as it was during his reign that India became independent from the British Empire, and the individual princely provinces were no longer recognized. Jawaharlal Nehru, independent India's first Prime Minister, gave these princely states three choices: join India, join Pakistan, or declare yourself a separate state. The third choice was not really a choice, the second one was not geographically possible for provinces not situated on India's northern periphery and also, almost all of them were Hindu sates and the question of joining Muslim Pakistan did not arise. Every principality south of Delhi opted to join India. The individual ruling families of Rajputana in western India joined together to form the state of Rajasthan, which was then incorporated into India as a regular state.

In 1945, just before independence, a young Englishwoman named Lillian Godfreda Luter escaped to India from the unrest in Burma where she had been teaching. At the very same time, Man Singh of Jaipur wanted to start an exclusive girls' school, mainly catering to princesses from the royal families of the neighboring principalities. Miss Luter had good credentials to be appointed as principal, and so MGD was born. The royal family donated the land and built the school, an impressive pink stone structure. A high compound wall ran on the periphery of acres and acres of school grounds, which was large enough to hold the actual school building, several hostel buildings on one end, Miss Luter's house on the other end, a building for residential teachers, a separate science complex, a small art studio, huge playgrounds in the front, and a swimming pool and sports track at the back.

In those early years of the school, students arrived in *purdah* so that no male eyes saw them. They wore white *salwars* with light blue *kurtas* that had a collar and a pocket to the top left on which MGD's monogram was embroidered in maroon, and a matching maroon *chunni* of georgette to cover their heads. The sleeves of the kurta were short and in the winter they wore maroon sweaters or blazers. MGD's uniform remained the same throughout the years, except that we did not drape the *chunnis* over our heads any more. We pinned it on our shoulder with pleats in the front covering our chests. On our feet we wore black leather naughty boy shoes that were rounded in the front and had laces and a solid sole, a concession to the very British Miss Luter who deemed that they were the most comfortable for school children to wear.

In July of 1973, when Shammi and I passed the entrance tests and officially became MGDians, Miss Luter was a tiny, plump, bent old lady who kept her peppery gray hair short, wore round rimless glasses, walked with the aid of a wooden cane, and wore skirt suits made of light cotton tailored in her native England. She always wore comfortable flat shoes, and on her left arm, just over her elbow, was a copper band worn for its medicinal properties. The skin around the band was a bluish green caused by sweat and metal, and in this band she would tuck in her handkerchief so it was handy for her to remove and wipe her forehead occasionally. She had a shrill voice, and spoke fluent Hindi with a very British accent.

"Ramiram," she would screech, calling for her trusted peon, "*Idhar Aao,*" and Ram-i-ram would come running from wherever he was. All the teachers of MGD respected Miss Luter, all the girls loved her, and all the servants adored her.

When Lillian Godfreda Luter fled Burma, she also took with her a young Burmese orphan girl whom she had been caring for, Emma. Miss Emma was Miss Luter's surrogate daughter, and by the time I joined the school, she too was the old Miss Emma in her Burmese sarong and a white sleeveless blouse. Her rapidly thinning hair was combed up and tightly knotted on the top of her head. Miss Emma was the official head of the administrative office of MGD and Miss Luter's "right-hand-man." Miss Emma was also the gateway to Miss Luter's office.

In the days before we joined MGD, as part of the preparation, Mummy sat us down once and said very seriously,

"The girls who come to MGD come from rich families. Some might come to school in chauffeur driven cars. They will talk of homes that are big and things that they have in those homes. You two do not have that. I am sending you to a more expensive school, and that is all I can afford now. So please do not compare yourselves to the other girls there."

This was a big decision for Mummy to make all alone. Just like she decided that she would not go to Bangalore, where all our relatives were, after Daddy died, but instead come to Jaipur where nobody knew her. And once she decided, she was firm and nobody could say anything. The tuition fee at MGD was considerably more than the convent we attended, but a year after starting her own nursery school she felt that she could afford that.

Shammi and I were part of a group called the day scholars—children who lived locally in Jaipur and who went home every evening. This group was different from the close-knit group of boarders who lived in one of the several hostels on the school grounds. They were away from their own families, and so MGD was their home. They had special after-school activities and special outings into the city. Almost all of them came from wealthy backgrounds, many of whose parents lived in Europe and America. These girls had "seen the world," and they walked around school with a special know-it-all attitude that I secretly envied.

We went to school in a tempo—a larger auto rickshaw with an elongated back—that could seat about twelve kids. The driver stopped in front of each girl's house, and on the way home from school took the same route in reverse again, dropping us off one at a time. If any of the girls were not ready and waiting in the mornings, he would honk loudly, a most displeasing sound to the ear, like a huge monster with a terribly bad throat and one that paid no attention to tone.

Even though Miss Luter was very British, the customs we followed at school were very Indian and very traditional. At the morning assembly in the quadrangle outside her office, the prayer was always in Sanskrit. Lighting of a huge *diya* and prayers preceded every school function. We celebrated all Hindu festivals religiously.

But at the same time, we were allowed a certain freedom that the Catholic nuns at St. Angela Sophia would not dream of. For starters, the teachers were called by their names. So it was "Good morning Mrs. Menon," or "How are you Miss Mehta?" and not Ma'am or Madam or just Miss. With Miss Luter's connections and the royal family's help, we had important visitors to the school on a regular basis, and in our senior years, if we were part of special clubs or were student leaders, we met them in small groups over tea and snacks.

I joined MGD at the age when puberty was just hitting us in our face, and the very bold attitude of the girls there was a big change. Menstrual periods were called "chums," and so it was, "Are you having your chums, *yaar*?" Because the uniform *kurtas* were loose fitting, how did one find out if a girl had started wearing a bra? You would thump her very hard on the back, even if she were not your friend—especially if she was not your friend—and say, "Hi, *yaar*," feeling for the bra strap in the process. Then you could pass the message to your own group about the bra situation. The word *yaar* loosely translates into "buddy" in proper English. It is a Hindi slang that has been incorporated into Indian English, and we said, "Come on, *yaar*," or "Don't worry, *yaar*," or "*Arre, yaar*," very easily and very often.

Saturdays in MGD were half-days, and they were also sports days. For this we had a separate uniform. We wore white shorts, white shirts with the MGD monogram embroidered in maroon again on the pocket, white socks, and white sneakers. As a concession to the sentiments of more conservative families, a student could wear white pleated divided skirts instead, but both Shammi and I loved the shorts. This sports uniform was definitely a later addition as I cannot imagine princesses in *purdah* running about the playing field in any type of western attire, fully covered or not.

The entire school was divided into four houses—we had the orange house named for Sarojini Naidu, a well-known Indian poetess, freedom fighter, and politician of the early twentieth century; we had the blue house named for Helen Keller; the green house named for Florence Nightingale; and the red house called Madame Curie. Each girl wore a pin on her collar of the color matching the house she was assigned to. In my senior year, I would become the co-captain of the red house, a position of some honor as one had to be voted to it by the girls. I wore two pins, one on each collar of my uniform, one proclaiming my house color and the other saying that I was a captain. Miss Luter held a very elaborate handing-over ceremony at the end of every year when the old captains handed over reigns to the captains-elect.

In 1970, a year before Daddy, Man Singh of Jaipur collapsed and died while playing polo in England and Gayatri Devi became the Rajmata or Queen Mother. She would come to MGD for all important occasions, and I would see her sitting in the front row with Miss Luter and the senior teachers. Graceful even in her middle age, she would always wear a French Chiffon sari in pastel shades and prints. As a true Rajput, she would always drape the *pulloo* of her sari over her head. The material was so thin that you could see her neatly coffered black hair that she would always wear in a shoulder-length bob. There was no make up on her face except for light lipstick on her lips that added to the beauty of her pale complexion. She never wore much jewelry, and when she spoke, her voice was deep and husky. Sometimes, when we practiced for our yearly sports meet, I would see her drive up to the field herself and watch the girls from a distance. On these days she would wear trousers and a thin short *kurta* on top, and I would be enamored. I was not a Rajput, I was certainly not from a royal family, and I did not have her fair skin. It was nice just to watch her.

Not once did Mummy regret sending her girls to MGD. Miss Luter instilled confidence and poise in her girls, and the teachers respected their individualities. Aparna's death was never spoken about openly at school. It was unfortunate that it had happened, but life had to go on. My classmates were girls from rich families, from royal families, from politicians' families, from film stars' families, and from ordinary families like mine. In school, we were one, no one person more special than the other.

Shammi and I did not become arrogant MGDians as people had warned Mummy because once we were home, we were Mummy's girls, and did exactly what she told. Just as we did not go to school in chauffeur driven cars, we did not have servants to wait on us at home. We took turns to clean the table after every meal, we ironed our own uniforms every weekend, polished our own shoes, and helped Mummy with dusting and cleaning and occasionally cooking.

By shifting us to MGD, Mummy had finally done something that Daddy's death had interrupted. He had wanted his girls to grow up smart and confident and independent, and now, by having us attend MGD, Mummy had achieved Daddy's dream, and she was confident that he was watching from above, approving her every move.

I met Rajmata Gayatri Devi one last time in 2004 when I went home to attend the 25th anniversary reunion of our high school batch. She shook hands with each of us who attended, and took the time to ask us how we were doing. Gayatri Devi died in the summer of 2009, a grand old lady of eighty-nine. An era of grandeur ended with her.

Raja Park

During the slow and uneventful times of my teenage years—when all the appropriate hormones for my age raged and rioted inside me—Raja Park was the heart of Tilak Nagar in Jaipur. Tilak Nagar was not like C-Scheme in uptown Jaipur where all the houses were big and the streets wide. Jewelers and the other business class lived in C-Scheme, while the middle-class lived in localities like Tilak Nagar, which was right next to the University campus. Even Tilak Nagar was divided into A, B, and C according to the lot sizes for each house, and ours was a "C," which meant that this was the smallest size. Raja Park was a half-mile stretch of street on one end of Tilak Nagar, which was flanked by shops and bakeries and road side *Dhabas*—which served hot and spicy tandoori chicken on cold winter nights—on either side. It was our very own Connaught Place, our very own Piccadilly, and our very own Georgetown, except back then, there were no pubs or bars in Raja Park. During the hot summer months, Raja Park was a ghost town during the day. Shops would either shut down during the afternoon hours or shopkeepers would cover the front of their stores with heavy tarpaulin to keep the blazing sunlight out, but in the evenings this marketplace came alive with shoppers from all the surrounding residential localities.

More than shopping, Raja Park grew into a sort of hanging out place for people of all ages. For the housewives, it was an outing after a full day of cooking, cleaning, and washing. This was the time they could get out of their houses with their husbands and children, and leave nagging in-laws behind. And then their joy and delight upon accidentally meeting another family would become evident by their loud chatter and easy laughter. Traffic in Raja Park had to move very slowly as you could at any time encounter such a group standing by the side of the street and socializing. For the younger male college crowd, Raja Park became a gathering place to just meet friends, sit on their motorbikes and sip coca cola from chilled bottles, or just smoke the evening away while ogling at girls.

I was never allowed to go to Raja Park with my friends just to "hang out." My mother would have none of that nonsense, and my only forays into the market place would be on a genuine errand or if I accompanied Mummy on one of her shopping trips. I had learnt to ride the scooter soon after Mummy had bought one a couple of years after starting her elementary school. After selling off our Ambassador sedan in Bombay, soon after Daddy's death, this was our first vehicle, and it made us very proud. Mummy let me take the scooter to Raja Park, and I was always willing to run errands for her, for it meant I would get to ride the light gray Bajaj with four gears. Soon I became an expert in weaving my way through the crowded streets of Jaipur.

Going to Raja Park also meant that I would go past all the boys lounging on their bikes, and I knew that a girl on a scooter would attract their attention. I could feel their eyes watching my every move. They watched as I slowed for traffic, and they watched as I stopped in front of a store and put the scooter on its stand. They also watched when I started the scooter with a kick. All the time I was careful not to look back at them, as I was not interested in any of them, but at the same time I was aware of their attention. I let them look at me and I enjoyed it. I lingered where I could have been quicker.

Of course, it also helped that all the shopkeepers in Raja Park, and lot of the people who shopped there, knew whose daughter I was. Mummy's school was becoming more popular with each passing year, and the local people had started recognizing us on the streets. Looking back on my teenage years, I am doubly sure now that I would never have entertained the idea of getting to know any of the boys hanging out in Raja Park. But vanity has its place, and I did want them to notice me. I certainly did nothing untoward to attract attention, so it was very rewarding to have it anyway. Now I know that Mummy sensed it and knew about it, but trusted me enough to never doubt my actions. Did Shammi feel the same way when she was growing up? I have never asked.

"Suppy, wash your face and comb your hair, we have to go to Raja Park." My mother insisted that we should always greet the evenings with a freshly washed face, and it really did not matter if we were going to Raja Park or not.

"My face is fine."

"I do not like oily faces." Mummy could be persistent. "And remember, an oily face means pimples."

Shammi and I had learnt that grumbling was of no use, so we dutifully washed our faces, combed our hair, and stood in front of Mummy to see her visible relief. Of course, Mummy too would wash her face, comb her hair, and even brush her teeth at the end of every hot afternoon, but over the years, I failed to see the point of it and did it just to please her. Too much of face washing removes the natural oils that the skin produces, I read in beauty magazines today, but we did not know it then, and it would not have mattered anyway. Mummy would have argued that there can be too much of the natural thing, and when it oozes out, we have to get rid of it.

If we had to go to Raja Park, face washing could not be disputed at all. Because most of the children in Mummy's elementary school came from the neighboring localities, our trip to Raja Park would invariably mean bumping into the parents of some of these children—anxious parents—who would waylay Mummy with all the problems their child was having on that given day. So we had to look our best, as Mummy could have no child of hers clumsily dressed.

"I *have* to be nice to them," Mummy would whisper fiercely when Shammi and I complained about this constant interruption just as we were about to enter a store. For every such meeting with a parent, we spent five or ten minutes standing dutifully by the side with a polite smile on our faces.

That half-mile stretch of market place that constituted Raja Park had no streetlights. There were enough stores bordering the street on either side with bright yellow bulbs and tube lights to light up the street outside. Shoppers could park their cars or scooters or bicycles or motorbikes just outside the store on a strip of dirt that lined the street on each side and then step on to a cemented pavement before stepping into the individual store. There were no lane markings on the street and no parking spaces as such. You parked wherever you found the space, even if it meant that you were blocking somebody else.

Like any other discerning shopper, Mummy patronized some stores more than the others. When we entered Raja Park, the second store on the right belonged to the Makhijas. Mummy bought falls for her saris from this middle-aged couple, and for a few rupees extra, they would even stitch the fall on to the sari and have it ready the next day. They sold other knick-knacks too, but we visited them only when we needed falls. And every time Mummy bought one, there would be the same conversation.

"We sell only the best quality falls, *Behenji*," Mr. Makhija would assure my mother. "It is the best cotton, and the color will not run. Even your silk saris are safe."

"There is no need to shrink these falls, *Behenji*." Mrs. Makhija would chime in. "They are made of pre-shrunk cotton." Five yards of this four-inch wide piece of cloth was of utmost importance to the well being of any sari. It was attached to the inside of the border on the bottom to protect the embroidered border and the edge of the sari and also to give the sari some weight so it would "fall" well.

Because the Makhijas also sold eggs and bread to supplement the income from their tiny store, Shammi and I called them "*Unda* Makhija," and sometimes we would even buy *undas* from them to make fluffy omelets for our dinner. It is funny how nomenclature becomes a way of life, and to this day, when I visit home, I say I am going to buy my sari falls from the *Unda* Makhijas. We can think of them as none other.

Out of habit, or convenience, or loyalty—whichever— Mummy insisted on buying all the vegetables from the first vegetable store on the left just beyond the *Unda* Makhijas. Maybe the habit formed from having to park the scooter only once and walking to all these stores to finish off buying whatever was on her shopping list. The vegetable store had huge round baskets of fresh greens, onions, potatoes, and seasonal vegetables lined on each side, and we could pick what we liked. The owner would sit way inside in front of huge iron scales surrounded by more baskets of vegetables all around him. His helper, a young boy, and by the looks of him, a close relative, would walk around sprinkling water on the vegetables to keep them looking fresh.

Mummy loved to bargain for the price of these vegetables.

"I can easily go to the *Mundi* and get these vegetables on wholesale price *Bhaiyya*," she would tell the man sitting cross-legged inside the store while selecting round and plump egg plants from a basket or breaking the tips of the okra deftly with her fingers to see if they were tender.

He would just smile and say, "Will I ever cheat you *Behenji*?" He knew and my mother knew that a trip to the *Mundi* in Jaipur's downtown was a trip she would not make. Neither did she have the time nor the inclination for such a trip, but buying the vegetables without bargaining for a few paisas less was unthinkable to a seasoned shopper. I soon learnt her bargaining style, and occasionally when I came to the market to get vegetables on her list, I would try it too. Somehow to me, it felt shallow and forced, and more than once I gave in to what the man quoted.

"I do hope you are not overcharging me," I would say, however, in a tone that conveyed confidence and maturity.

The vegetable man would always laugh and say, "I do not cheat your mother, why will I cheat you?"

And then I learnt from Mummy to always ask for *masaala* while he was weighing our purchases. This consisted of a bunch of coriander leaves and a handful of green chilies with maybe a lemon or two, which the vegetable man was expected to give us free as a bonus for buying the vegetables from him. You had to ask for the extra topping with an air of authority so that he immediately complied without questioning the demand.

There were two good bakeries in Raja Park, and it was always a dilemma for us to decide where to buy our favorite snacks with our evening tea on occasional weekends—patties and pineapple pastries. Paljee's identical twin daughters studied in Mummy's school and so did Bakewell's grandson. Finally we decided unanimously that Paljee made the best meat and vegetable patties and Bakewell had the better pastry. We bought bread from either place depending on which bakery we were closer to that day.

The one item that Mummy never let us buy by ourselves was sanitary pads. She always bought that for us, and the storekeeper would wrap the packet with old newspaper and tie it with a string before handing it to us—as if it were a secret pact between us, and he felt very important to be privy to this personal bit of information.

Just opposite Paljee's bakery was Beauty Corner, which sold all types of cosmetics and creams. It was a wonderful store to browse through, except that I took a deep dislike to the man who sat behind the counter. He had a special uncomfortable way of looking at young girls, though his manner and speech were most courteous and polite. Mummy knew this, and I always went into that store only when she was with us. Whenever we went in, he would make it a point to tell us that he had a fresh stock of fancy bras and undergarments, which we never bought from him. We went there just for the latest colors in Lakmé nail polish and lipsticks or Emami talcum powder or deep cleansing cream for the face.

Often, when I stepped out of Paljee's bakery, I would see the Beauty Corner man sitting idly outside his store, and he would nod a greeting to me from across the street inviting me in to see the latest. I took great pleasure in ignoring him and his nod. His behavior never changed as he advanced in age. Years later, after I was engaged and then married to Anil, I would complain about the Beauty Corner fellow, and Anil would just laugh and tease me.

"Don't be silly, he's a nice man. He offers me the latest brand in imported condoms whenever I go to that store. And they are in beautiful pastels..." Anil would say this and laugh out loud at the look of horror and disgust on my face. The Beauty Corner man knew that I was Anil's wife, and that made me feel all the more uncomfortable. The only logical thing to do was to forbid Anil from ever stepping into that store.

And that was just one more thing about all the shopkeepers in Raja Park. Because Anil's house was in the next street from ours, the moment we got engaged, all of them knew. Anil's family also shopped at these very same stores, and I felt connected to all these people in two ways. Mummy bought all her monthly groceries from one store, while my mother-in-law did her shopping from another store. During the years I was engaged to Anil, I could walk into any of these stores and get special attention, and it made me feel nice.

On my yearly trips home to Jaipur now, I still shop in Raja Park. It has become a busy marketplace, and more people drive cars than scooters, and parking is a nightmare. Mummy has a snazzy Hyundai now, and when Shammi and I go shopping, we step out of the car instead of putting the scooter on its stand. Raja Park has the latest in footwear these days, and it has air-conditioned showrooms where I can try out sandals and slippers.

At Bakewell, the son has taken over the business, and I see the grandfather only occasionally. Whenever I meet him I fold my hands and say *Namaste*.

"*Beti*, it is nice of you to remember us after all your years in America," he says and enquires after Anil and the boys. He lost his wife to cancer a few years back, and whenever he comes to the store now, he just sits in one place and supervises.

Paljee's bakery continues to sell the best patties, and the only change is in Paljee's face. He has grown old prematurely after the death of his only son in an accident. His twin daughters are both married, he tells me, and he is a grandfather. When he looks at my boys, I wonder if he is remembering his lost son.

And whenever I walk out of Paljee, I see Mr. Beauty Corner, and see that he has grown old too. I do not go there. I do not buy nail enamels and lipstick and creams in India these days. Mrs. *Unda* Makhija has lost all her front teeth, and has not bothered to get dentures so her face sags even more. Mr. Makhija just has a few extra grays in his hair. I don't buy too many saris, but whenever Mummy presents me with one, I go there for the fall, and they are genuinely thrilled to see me.

Raja Park is no longer the one half-mile stretch of market. It has spread to other lanes surrounding it, and I do not know many of the stores. What is important is that the ones I knew are still there, and I feel a true sense of homecoming when I visit them. I see young boys hanging out on their motorbikes even now. They have become smarter and better looking and better dressed, but to me they are kids. I feel their eyes on Shammi and me as we step out of our car smartly dressed in our designer jeans and tops and not looking our age, but I know that they know that we really are much older. My oldest son accompanies me on some of these trips, and I feel proud to have a young man next to me who towers over me. I meet people whom I do not know, but they smile at us, as they know that we are Mrs. Satyan's daughters.

Color

"Why don't you marry the younger sister? She is lighter in color."

This was Anil's grandmother's reaction when he told her that if he would be married at all, it would be only to me. Color was a big part of Nani*ji*'s life, and she was obsessed with it. She liked the color white, and it showed as even her bed linen was always pure white, and she had it starched stiff so that any dirt on it would wash off when it was laundered next. Spoken like a true North Indian, I thought when Anil told me this, very hesitatingly, a few months after we got engaged. He was quick to assure me, of course, that none of his other family members shared his grandmother's opinion. *They* did not comment on the "color" of a person's skin, especially that of a girl's. Nani*ji* did have a point though. I was entering a family where everyone was much lighter in complexion than I was, and I felt that I was darkening their collective gene pool.

Being dark in color was sort of self-explanatory when everyone found out that Anil was marrying a South Indian. We are the Dravidians, the original inhabitants of India who got pushed further to the south all those thousands of years back with each onslaught of invading Aryans from the North. The Aryans came from the northwest with their lighter skin tones, and established the general belief, whether true or not, that North Indians have lighter skin colors than the South Indians. Color has become so ingrained in people's minds in India that the idea of beauty has a direct correlation to the color of the skin. My mother inherited her father's darker skin tone instead of my grandmother's lighter color, and I was born with a sort of halfway color, a mix of hers and my father's much lighter skin. Mummy was upset that I did not have Daddy's complexion.

"Who will marry my daughter?" she had pouted a few months after my birth, when a baby's true color is established.

"Didn't I marry you?" My father had teased. "There will be plenty of boys lined up to marry my daughter."

Daddy was like Anil. Detested anyone who talked about how dark-skinned or how white somebody was unless it was appreciatively. Mummy loves to tell us about a business trip that Daddy returned from and told her that the beautiful film actress, Waheeda Rehman, was traveling in the same airplane as him. Mummy became terribly excited and asked him to describe what she looked like in person. "Chocolate colored, and equally appetizing," he retorted, making Mummy very jealous. I would have loved to see his reaction to Mrs. Rastogi, our loud neighbor in Jaipur, who would stand on her side of the low compound wall that separated our two houses and tell Mummy,

"Mrs. Bhargav down the street is very lucky. Her new daughter-in-law is very beautiful, "*gori, chitti*," much more light-skinned than anyone in their family. Now look at our poor Uma," and she would point her hefty arms at the house opposite ours, "they have not found a boy for her because she is so dark, just like a *Madraasi*."

It would take supreme control on Mummy's part not to retaliate verbally to a remark like that. Everyone around us labeled us *Madraasi*, hailing from Madras, even though the South is divided into many different states. It was no use telling them that we were from Bangalore in the state of Karnataka and not every South Indian was from Madras in Tamil Nadu, and of course also that just because you are from Madras does not mean that you should be dark in color. "These people need a lesson in geography," Mummy would grumble later on to Shammi and me.

"Mrs. Rastogi, not every South Indian is dark in color. Just as there are dark-skinned North Indians, there are very light-skinned South Indians. You have seen my sister Rama; now isn't she very light-skinned?" Mummy's explanation would fall on deaf ears, while Mrs. Rastogi started off about some other family in the neighborhood.

"It does not matter if you are dark or light-skinned," Mummy would tell Shammi and me when we entered our teenage years, "it is the quality of the skin that is important." We dutifully dabbed our faces with cotton balls dipped in cleansing milk to wash away the hidden dust and grime in our pores, and applied a thick layer of night cream. We were careful not to rub the delicate skin around our eyes, and applied a little castor oil to our eyelashes and eyelids to keep them supple and soft. Soap is bad for the facial skin, I was told, so I washed my face with a paste made of gram flour and water. Now, I use ready made face washes with micro beads that exfoliate the skin with each wash. The gram flour did the same thing. You could feel its roughness on the face, and sometimes I would add a pinch of turmeric to it to see if it really made my skin color any different. After all, on the radio they did advertise *Vico Turmeric Ayurvedic Cream*, a skin cream that promised a light and radiant complexion, and they did say that it had turmeric in it. In commercials that were shown in theatres before the start of a movie, they showed brides preparing for their big day by applying daily treatments of this cream.

Shammi and I never used it. Common sense told us that nothing in the world could change the basic color of the skin's pigment. No amount of scrubbing would make my arms look any lighter in color than what they were. Secretly, though, I did always wonder why God had not made me at least two shades lighter. I would stare at myself in the mirror and imagine what I would have looked like if I had been "whiter." I would regularly wax my arms as I realized that even removing what little hair I had there, made the skin brighter. And the only people I could voice my concerns to were my friends in college during our regular beauty secrets discussion.

"You know, Supriya, when a person is very "white," the features do not show through as well," Rani, my very light-skinned friend told me and this assured me greatly. If I ever told Mummy about my concerns with color, she would start off on a big sermon about how maintaining my body was more important than worrying about what I could not have.

"If you still want to wear jeans and *salwars* and *churidars* when you are forty, then you should not become fat after marriage and maintain yourself." That was her only worry for us, and she would not miss any chance to point that out. She did not want Shammi and me to let go and become shapeless. "Now look at that Aparna Bhatnagar," another South Indian woman who had married a Bhatnagar, like I would later, and would walk around our neighborhood with tight fitting clothes that showed off her great figure, "she has two kids and it does not show at all."

To this day, when I visit home, Mummy gives me a good look-over after the initial hug of greeting to see how much or how little I have changed, and she feels a sense of achievement and pride if I look "the same." Shammi was born with our father's light skin, and that was what made her more appealing to Anil's grandmother. Naniji's obsession with light-colored skin was lifelong, and we all knew it and joked about it too. By looking at old photographs I could make out that Anil's grandfather was not particularly white in color, but her idea of whiteness applied only to the female members in her family. Her daughter and then her granddaughter were born with milky white complexions, and that is all that mattered. When she went to "see" a prospective bride for her son, the clever family dressed the girl in such a way that only her face showed and it was a heavily made-up face. So Naniji ended up with a daughter-in-law who did not match up to her standards of whiteness. And then, even her grandson married someone who was not "white" in color.

"Nani*ji*, I do not want the younger sister, I want to marry Suppy," Anil had told his grandmother sternly when she had reacted to his decision. I never resented her for this remark as she was a grand old lady, set in her ways, very frank in her opinions, but genuine nonetheless. Once I joined the family, she promptly forgot about the color of my skin and accepted me wholeheartedly.

In America now, there is no difference in Anil's skin color or mine. It is the same. Neither is there any difference between my very light-skinned cousin and my much darker-skinned cousin. We are all Indians and we are all the same—brown. And that is a very important distinction, at least for us. North Indians and South Indians become one here, and even the Indians themselves do not care. Skin color was the only indication to my children when they entered pre-school that they were different. Each of them had one day when they realized they were not white, they were not black, but they were brown, and they came home and told me this as if they had made a big discovery.

"Tara*ji*, your grandsons were born in America, yet they are not *gora, chitta*." Mrs. Rastogi remarked loudly to my mother each time I took my boys home during summer breaks. And then she would look at me and say, "Suppy, you did not eat right during your pregnancy. If you had had enough of... (and here she would go off on a list of food items that I had never heard of) then your boys would have been more *gora*."

Mummy has long given up on her neighbor, and explained to her patiently that just being born in the west does not make one's skin turn white.

"They are so thin," Mrs. Rastogi would continue. "Does not look as if they have come from America. Rastogi *Saab's* brother's son was born in Canada, and you should see him—white as milk and with well rounded arms and legs."

This would be a cue to us that this was a pointless conversation, and we would hurry with our goodbyes and rush indoors. No point explaining to her that by the time I go home each summer, my boys have played enough in the hot sun outside to thoroughly tan their brown skins. Sometimes, when they were younger, I would be tempted to tell them not to play outside or go to the swimming pool before our trip, as I did not want that tan when I went home to show them off. I wanted the people there, especially nosey neighbors, to see their true color. But on second thoughts, I attributed that impulse to extremely unreasonable thinking, and dared not voice it aloud for fear that Anil would laugh at me.

As my children grow, I find myself dwelling not so much on the color of their skin but more on their health, their education, and their future. I continue to do everything, however, to prevent my skin from tanning to a darker color, even if it means holding an umbrella over my head on hot summer days. This only produces protests from Anil and lots of "Mamma, please do not embarrass us," from my boys, but I do not listen to them. I see to it that I sit only in shaded spots when we go to the pool, and only under huge trees when we picnic in a park. Despite all this, like a chameleon, my skin changes shades, and just feeling the heat of the sun is enough to make it darker.

The one time when I truly did not bother about the color of my skin was during my pregnancies. Hormonal changes in the body caused the pigmentation of my skin to go haywire, and my skin became very dark in patches. But the joy of knowing that I had my children inside me made me forget how I looked, and when I look at them now I remember Daddy's words about how appetizing the color brown is.

Anil and I

Even though it has been more than thirty years now, I remember Anil's first kiss. We were on the terrace of his house—this was when all the neighboring houses were still single storied, and people had not sold off their houses to developers who promptly built tall apartment buildings—as this was the only place in the house where we could have some privacy. Anil put his arms around me and kissed me on the cheek whispering "I love you" softly in my ear. I quickly wiggled out of his arms and moved away saying, "I have to ask Mummy."

"Ask her what?" was Anil's surprised reaction. "I don't want to know if *she* loves me, I want to know if *you* love me."

"I have to ask Mummy," I repeated like a parrot.

Try as I might, I do not remember what happened next. I do know that I rushed home after promising Anil that I shall have an answer the next day. When I look back on this conversation, I realize that I never gave Anil a chance to propose marriage to me. The minute he declared his love for me, I told him that I would marry him, and when I remind him about that now, he jokes that he was fooled into marriage with me.

I was a few months past my seventeenth birthday and Anil had just finished his twenty-first that winter evening on the terrace, and even though I knew Anil liked me, his declaration of love confused me. No man had ever put his arms around me like that and kissed me. After my father's death there were many uncles who gave me hugs, but my uncles never kissed, and a man's lips on my face was something new.

111

I do not remember how old I was when I "saw" Anil for the first time. His house was in the next lane from ours in Tilak Nagar, and Mummy knew his mother through mutual acquaintances. I used to see a tall and thin boy with hair worn a little long and a big moustache go past our house on the scooter, and soon we found out that this was her son. He would drive by very fast, the wind blowing his hair back, and his body would always be slightly tilted on the scooter—not at a perfect right angle to the seat. I knew more about Anil's family than I did about him then. I knew that his father taught English at the University and that his mother taught History there. I knew that he had a sister in high school, a year younger than I was. And I knew that he had a grandmother living with them. What I did not know was that they had two dogs and a blind cat also.

Mummy was never overly protective of Shammi and me, and we were free to talk to anyone, even boys, as we were growing up. Even though we went to an all-girls school and then later to an all-girls college, there were many family friends who had sons, and we were good friends. There was Rohit in the house diagonally opposite ours and Madan in the house next to his. Both were a year older than me and both were my "friends." When I see my older son talk to my friends' daughters, I think of my teenage years in Jaipur. What will happen twenty years from now? Will he still be a friend to these girls? Will all of them have families of their own, move far away from each other, and forget that they grew up together?

Anil was a little older than Rohit and Madan, and back then, he looked older than his age, and that was what attracted me to him. And of course the fact that he was completely enamored by me and showed it added to the charm. I sensed it the first time I met him. Mummy had sent me over to his house to hand over an invitation to his mother, and I could hear the dogs barking the minute I rang the doorbell. Soon, Anil opened the door carrying the black mixed breed, Kalu, under one arm and the white Samoyed, Fluffy, under the other. I was face to face with all three of them at once, and they were adorable. At least Kalu and Anil. I am not so sure about Fluffy—we never formed a close bond, and it became the family joke later on that I had to worry more about Fluffy accepting me into the family rather than my mother-in-law.

Many years later, I found out that Anil had told his family that it was their future daughter-in-law who stood at the door that day. His parents had had a fairy tale romance when they first met, and this was not something new for them. They did not like the word "arranged," and it never occurred to them that they would have to find a bride for their son. When Anil had told his father that he wanted to marry me, his father had replied, "You have to marry the girl. Do not expect us to go ask her."

It was different in my family, however. As Mummy and Daddy's marriage was arranged, and because of the absence of a father in my life, my Uncle—Mummy's older brother—had started thinking of prospective grooms for me. It was all too early of course as there was no way Mummy was marrying me off before I finished my college education, but there was no harm in keeping "an eye out," as the elders in my family put it. On one summer trip to Bangalore, these elders persuaded my mother to have me meet one of the "prospective" grooms. I had protested, saying that I was not some saleable item that had to be held up for display, but not only was I too young, even my mother was too young to go against the wishes of her relatives. None of this would have happened if Daddy had been alive, I realized later. I would still be a baby in his eyes, and the remote possibility of "keeping an eye out" would not have happened. His death had made me grow up much sooner than I normally would have, and at sixteen and seventeen, I was all grown up.

The "prospective groom" I met that summer day in Bangalore was an Engineer from England, an Indian, whose twin brother was a graduate of the London School of Economics—I was told—and I liked the way he talked in his clipped British accent. I did not meet him again after that day, and I found out much later that he had asked if he could take me out on a date. My grandmother's brother and his wife, who were arranging the whole match, would have nothing of that so that had put an end to any further development in the relationship right away.

Now, I wonder what would have happened if they had agreed to let me go out with that boy. Would I have been married to him instead of Anil? Maybe I would be living in England now rather than in America. Maybe I would be the mother of three girls instead of three boys. These thoughts flash through my mind only occasionally, and they are gone the minute they enter. I can think of no other life than the one I am now living.

That attempt at an arranged marriage was the only one, as very soon after that Anil entered the scene. He was not an Iyengar from South India like us, but Mummy liked his family, and his parents did not care where I was from anyway. We were Brahmins, the priestly class, and his mother was an Aggarwal Baniya from the state of Punjab while his father was a Kayasth from Rajasthan, but that did not matter either. My mother and his parents were above all that. Caste did not matter. We were both Hindus, and I think Mummy cared more for that, even more than Anil's parents did.

"Suppy, I really do not think caste matters," she would tell me as I was growing up. "But I do think religion matters. It is very difficult for a girl to adjust in a family that is not Hindu." I never contradicted her then, but I do not agree with her now. Why should religion matter? Why cannot there be two religions in a family? When my boys grow up and one of them wants to marry an Indian who is not a Hindu, will I say no? Should I not be happy that he is marrying an Indian, whether Hindu or Muslim or Christian or Sikh? And then, what choice do I have anyway? Living here in America, what if he does not marry an Indian? Will I not let him decide and respect that decision, just like Anil's parents did?

In the early years of our courtship and marriage, Anil liked to tease me that there were many "matches" for him from rich Punjabi business families.

"And they were much lighter in color than me I suppose?" I would retort back. "All of those dumb females with just money and nothing else," I muttered under my breath. "Why did you marry me anyway?"

"Because I love only you," he would reply with a passion in his eyes that even I was not capable of.

That day, when I went home and told Mummy that Anil wanted to marry me, I put her in a quandary too. Her reply would map the course for the rest of my life, and I think she truly missed Daddy then. This was something she and I had to decide on our own. Nobody could help us, so we were up most of the night making a list of all the pros and cons of marrying Anil. The list of positives, of course, became larger than the negatives. On that latter side was only the fact that he was not an Iyengar, and having lived in the north all my life, I had no problem with that. I came from a Tamil speaking family, but spoke Hindi fluently, and knew all their customs and traditions. And then, I pointed out to my mother, Anil's family was least bothered with customs and traditions anyway. They were not like the others around us. They were educated and progressive in their thinking, and secretly I loved the fact that I would have a mother-in-law who works outside of the home. In my teenage mind was the thought that such women would make better mothers-in-law, and I lost no opportunity to point this out to Anil later on.

"If I hadn't liked your mother, I would never have said yes to you," I would tell him, especially after one of the many arguments and fights we had in those early years.

It was only after Anil and I were officially "engaged" that I was allowed to go out with him. He was studying in another city then, and we could meet only on his breaks home, and as this coincided with my breaks it gave us many free days to spend together. I have fond memories of eating out or going to the early morning shows of English movies. And now when Anil went past my house on his scooter, I would be on it too, riding the pillion seat sideways, my arms tightly around his waist, my chin on his right shoulder, my body touching his. I loved the smell of Old Spice, his after-shave, and it was a familiar and strangely comforting smell as Daddy had used it everyday. The wind would blow his hair onto my face, and on cold winter days, I would slip my arms under his jacket and love the warmth of his body against mine.

Apart from these outings to a restaurant or to see a movie, the only places we met were at his house or mine. I had become a part of his family and he of mine. We ate meals at each other's houses and interacted with each other's families. In Anil's house, I helped with the meals, and cleaned up after them. Occasionally, our families would leave us alone, but never for too long.

"I have a responsibility towards your mother," my future mother-in-law would say. "I have to protect her daughter from my son." So if we were ever in Anil's room for too long, either talking or just cuddling, she would find a reason to interrupt us.

"Mummy please do not be so obvious," Anil would tell his mother and she would just laugh and say it was her duty.

My sons have not brought home girls yet. I do not think they are old enough yet, but I know that is not true. I ask them about the girls in their school, but I am careful and try to be very tactful about it. They know what I am getting at, and just laugh off my questions. We have reached a stage in our relationship now, where we are more than mother and sons; we are friends. Of course, when it comes to studies and discipline and personal hygiene, I am still their mother, but when it comes to trust and emotional feelings, I try to be their mentor. I try to do what Anil's mother did with her son because I know that it worked. Anil is a devoted husband and father, and over the years has remained a devoted son, which I admire.

Almost three years of engagement—which my mother insisted upon as both of us had to finish our education—and twenty-eight years of marriage add up to thirty-one years, which is a big portion of my life so far. The edges of memory fade out and lose their sharpness. It is difficult for me to think of the time when I did not know Anil or those early years, after our engagement, when I was getting to know him. Even as I write this, he is fast asleep on our bed, snoring loudly. Our boys are in their rooms, asleep also, and if I try to think of a particular time in the past, I have to remind myself that it did exist. I have spent more of my life with Anil than with my mother, and this is my life now. *This* is my home, and *this* is my family.

Acknowledgment

I am greatly indebted to all the wonderful teachers in the MFA Program at George Mason University. Their guidance, along with the mentoring of all the visiting writers who came to GMU during my MFA days, was invaluable.

I would like to thank the wonderful publications staff at AWP for their excellent suggestions and help with the design and copyediting of the book.

My heartfelt thanks goes to the editors of Serving House Books for showcasing my work.

And last but not least, my family and friends have always been a great source of encouragement.